JEWISH LEARNING INSTITUTE

Soul Quest

The Journey Through Life, Death, and Beyond

Course Author
Rabbi Yisrael Rice

Soul Quest Editorial Team
Dr. Chana Silberstein, Editor-in-chief
Rabbi Mordechai Dinerman
Rabbi Yossi Nemes
Mr. Yaakov Ort
Rabbi Yossi Paltiel
Rabbi Sholom Raichik
Rabbi Shraga Sherman
Rabbi Avraham Sternberg

Printed in Canada
© Published and Copyrighted 2009 by
The Rohr Jewish Learning Institute
822 Eastern Parkway, Brooklyn, NY 11213

(888) YOUR-JLI/718-221-6900
www.myJLI.com

The **Rohr Jewish Learning Institute**
gratefully acknowledges
the pioneering support of

George and Pamela Rohr

SINCE ITS INCEPTION
the **Rohr JLI** has been
a beneficiary of the vision, generosity,
care and concern
of the **Rohr family**

In the merit of
the tens of thousands of hours of Torah study
by **JLI** students worldwide,
may they be blessed with health,
Yiddishe Nachas from all their loved ones,
and extraordinary success
in all their endeavors ❧

תְּנוּ לָהּ מִפְּרִי יָדֶיהָ וִיהַלְלוּהָ בַשְׁעָרִים מַעֲשֶׂיהָ _{משלי לא,לא}

This course is lovingly dedicated to the memory of

Mrs. Charlotte Rohr

on the occasion of her second *Yahrtzeit*

י׳ מרחשון תש״ע

MarCheshvan 10, 5770

October 28, 2009

לזכות האשה החשובה והיקרה

מרת **שרה** ע״ה

בת ר׳ יקותיאל יהודה ומרת לאה הי״ד

תנצב״ה

Table of Contents

Lesson 1
Who Am I?

Introduction

Think of your most cherished dream for the future. I don't know what your dream is, but I know you have the power to help it come true.

Because you have the ability to create, to invent, to love and to know. You have the freedom to choose a course in life that will make a real difference. All these powers comes from one place—the soul. The soul is the source of all change, all art, all inspiration, all love, and everything that makes us human.

What exactly is the soul? How can you get in touch with it? How can you access the power of your soul to change yourself and the world around you for the better?

We will explore all of this in Lesson One of *Soul Quest.*

Who Am I?

Text 1

כתיב (איוב י,יא): "עור ובשר תלבישני וגו'", בשרא דאדם לבושא איהו ובכל אתר כתיב בשר אדם; אדם לגו בשר לבושא דאדם גופא דיליה

זוהר א כ,ב

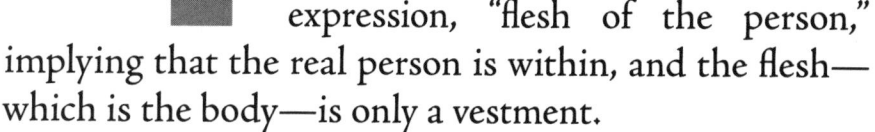

"You clothe me in skin and flesh (Iyov/Job 10:11)." We often encounter the expression, "flesh of the person," implying that the real person is within, and the flesh—which is the body—is only a vestment.

RABBI SHIMON BAR YOCHAI, ZOHAR I, 20B

Optional Section

Text 2

I turned in to Bograchov Street . . . . Then it happened. Suddenly, I felt a violent blow strike my head. I fell flat on the ground in front of the woman. A heavy, eighteen-foot wooden beam, plunging from the scaffold atop the five-story structure, hit me and I sailed into the street as if thrown by a catapult.

All at once, I felt I was outside my body, floating upward about twelve to fifteen feet above the sidewalk, watching the scene below. I did not know how I left my body, or how I got up there. Everything happened so suddenly that I was caught completely by surprise. I saw the large woman bending over my body, trying to detect a sign of life in my motionless form. Then she started screaming for help.

This is my body, I thought, but I am not inside it. I am looking at it from above. How is this possible? With what eyes am I seeing this, and where are my ears? How could I be hearing all this noise in the street?

I was baffled. Obviously, I existed, I was real, I was conscious, but not inside my frame. I always thought that "I" and my body were identical. I did not know I was a being that was more than just a physical body.

RACHEL NOAM, THE VIEW FROM ABOVE

What Is the Soul?

Learning Activity 1

In three words or less, try to define or describe the soul. For example, you might say, "source of life." You may write more than one answer, but no answer may be longer than three words.

Text 3a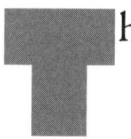

נפש כל בשר היא צורתו שנתן לו הא-ל

משנה תורה, הלכות יסודי התורה ד,ח

The soul of all flesh is the design that G-d gave it.

Rambam (Maimonides),
Mishneh Torah, Hilchot Yesodei HaTorah 4:8

Text 3b

והדעת היתרה המצויה בנפשו של אדם היא צורת האדם השלם בדעתו, ועל צורה זו נאמר בתורה "נעשה אדם בצלמנו כדמותנו" (בראשית א,כו) כלומר שתהיה לו צורה היודעת ומשגת הדעות שאין להם גולם כמו המלאכים שהם צורה בלא גולם עד שידמה להן, ואינו אומר על צורה זו הניכרת לעינים שהיא הפה והחוטם והלסתות ושאר רושם הגוף שזו תואר שמה, ואינה הנפש המצויה לכל נפש חיה שבה אוכל ושותה ומוליד ומרגיש ומהרהר, אלא הדעה שהיא צורת הנפש . . .

אין צורת הנפש הזאת מחוברת מן היסודות כדי שתפרד להם, ואינה מכח הנשמה עד שתהא צריכה לנשמה כמו שהנשמה צריכה לגוף, אלא מאת ה' מן השמים היא, לפיכך כשיפרד הגולם שהוא מחובר מן היסודות ותאבד הנשמה מפני שאינה מצויה אלא עם הגוף וצריכה לגוף בכל מעשיה לא תכרת הצורה הזאת, לפי שאינה צריכה לנשמה במעשיה, אלא יודעת ומשגת הדעות הפרודות מן הגולמים ויודעת בורא הכל ועומדת לעולם ולעולמי עולמים, הוא שאמר שלמה בחכמתו "וישוב העפר על הארץ כשהיה והרוח תשוב אל האלהים אשר נתנה" (קהלת יב,ז)

משנה תורה, הלכות יסודי התורה ד,ח-ט

he design of the human being is the extra intelligence found in the human soul of the person who is complete in his intelligence.

Regarding this design, it is said in the Torah: "Let Us make man in Our image and Our likeness (Bereishit/Genesis 1:26)." That means the human design is one that knows and grasps ideas that have no physical substance.

Thus, the human soul does not refer to the physical organs of the body, such as the mouth, nose, and other organs; nor does it refer to the basic vital soul that is found in every animate creature which eats and drinks and reproduces and feels and thinks . . . .

The form of the human soul is this intelligence [and ability to grasp the abstract] . . . .

The [human] soul comes from G-d in Heaven. Therefore, when the body, which is composed of the elements, decomposes, and the vital soul is lost, since it is only found together with the body which it needs for all its actions, the [human soul] is not cut off, for it does not need the [vital] soul for its actions. Rather, it knows and grasps intelligence which is not physical. It knows the Creator of all, and it endures forever. This is what Shlomo/Solomon said in his wisdom: "The dust returns to the earth, as it was, and the spirit returns to G-d who gave it (Kohelet/Ecclesiastes 12:7)."

I B I D . ,   4 : 8 - 9

Table **1.1**

Qualities of the (Uniquely) Human Soul According to Maimonides
Capable of comprehending the non-physical and abstract
Capable of knowing G-d
Metaphysical
Eternal

Rabbi Yitschak Luria (1534–1572). Known by the acronym AriZal or simply the Ari. Founder of the Lurianic school of Kabbalah. Born in Jerusalem; raised in Egypt; died in Safed. Rabbi Luria studied Talmud under Rabbi Betzalel Ashkenazi, compiler of the *Shitah Mekubetzet*. Despite his youth, he was accepted among the rabbinic elite of Safed. The *Ari* never recorded his teachings; they were collected and transcribed by his disciples. His leading disciple, Rabbi Chaim Vital, is generally considered the most authoritative recorder of the AriZal's teachings. His primary work is his *Eitz Chaim*.

Text 4

כי הנשמה חלק אלו-ה ממעל והיא מתאוה תמיד לעלות אל בית אביה
לקוטי תורה, בראשית

The soul is a part of G-d from above and it desires constantly to rise up to its "Father's house."

Rabbi Yitschak Luria, Likutei Torah, Bereishit

Origin and Purpose of the Soul

Text 5a

וַיִּיצֶר ה׳ אֱלֹקִים אֶת הָאָדָם עָפָר מִן הָאֲדָמָה וַיִּפַּח בְּאַפָּיו נִשְׁמַת חַיִּים
וַיְהִי הָאָדָם לְנֶפֶשׁ חַיָּה

בראשית ב,ז

And HaShem Elokim formed the human of soil from the earth, and breathed into his nostrils the breath of life; and man became a living soul.

BEREISHIT 2:7

Text 5b

וַיֹּאמֶר אֱלֹקִים תּוֹצֵא הָאָרֶץ נֶפֶשׁ חַיָּה לְמִינָהּ בְּהֵמָה וָרֶמֶשׂ וְחַיְתוֹ אֶרֶץ לְמִינָהּ
וַיְהִי כֵן

בראשית א,כד

And Elokim said, "Let the earth bring forth all kinds of living souls according to their kind, cattle, and creeping things, and beasts of the earth according to their kind," and it was so.

IBID., 1:24

Text 5c

Rabbi Shne'ur Zalman of Liadi (1745–1812). Known as "the Alter Rebbe" and "the Rav"; Born in Liozna, Belarus; buried in Hadiach, Ukraine; chassidic Rebbe and founder of the Chabad movement; among the principal students of the Magid of Mezeritch. His numerous works include the *Tanya,* an early classic of Chassidism; *Torah Or* and *Likutei Torah*; and *Shulchan Aruch HaRav,* a rewritten code of Jewish law. He was succeeded by his son, Rabbi Dovber of Lubavitch.

The human body was created from the lowest element, the inanimate. The reason for this is that the human carries out the ultimate purpose of creation. This purpose is the elevation of sparks of G-dliness that have descended into our world. We achieve this elevation through utilizing the various aspects of this world, for example, eating food and wearing clothes. And then the person serves G-d, and this service is made possible through the material objects of this world.

In order to lift something properly, one needs to place their grip below the entire object. We see this clearly with a lever, which is placed totally under the object one wishes to lift. So too, the material that G-d used to create man was of the lowest form, so that man could successfully lift it back to its source.

BASED ON RABBI SHNE'UR ZALMAN OF LIADI, TORAH OR 4A

The Soul as an Interface
The Translator

Text 6

aria speaks only Spanish. David speaks only English. They are incompatible. They each have information, life experience, and thoughts which they can give to others and receive from others. However, Maria and David cannot speak with each other. There can be little interchange of knowledge, feeling, or experience.

Their inability to communicate may not bother you, until you learn that David is Maria's grandson. The rich life of Maria is a closed book to David. And David's exciting youth remains a mystery to Maria. She yearns to understand him, but cannot. There is a language barrier.

The solution is a translator. This is the purpose of an interface. A person who knows English and Spanish will be able to create a bridge between these two people who are so close, but yet, so far.

RABBI YISRAEL RICE

Experiencing the Soul

Text 7

כגון ד״מ האוכל בשרא שמינא דתורא ושותה יין מבושם להרחיב דעתו לה׳
ולתורתו כדאמר רבא חמרא וריחא כו׳ (יומא עו,ב) או בשביל כדי לקיים
מצות ענג שבת וי״ט אזי נתברר חיות הבשר והיין שהיה נשפע מקליפת נוגה
ועולה לה׳ כעולה וכקרבן

תניא פרק ז

f one eats fat beef and drinks spiced wine not out of
physical desire, but in order to broaden the mind
for the service of G-d and for His Torah, as Rava
said, "Wine and fragrance make my mind more receptive (Talmud Yoma 76b)," or in order to fulfill the com-
mandment to enjoy the Sabbath and the festivals, then,
the vitality of the meat and the wine . . . ascends to G-d
like a burnt offering and sacrifice [i.e., the life force that
the food and drink contain is absorbed in sanctity].

RABBI SHNE'UR ZALMAN OF LIADI, TANYA, CHAPTER 7

Table 1.2

בָּרוּךְ אַתָּה ה'
אֱלֹ-הֵינוּ מֶלֶךְ הָעוֹלָם
שֶׁהַכֹּל נִהְיָה בִּדְבָרוֹ

The *Brachah*	
Baruch	**Drawing down**
Atah	**You,** This is the way that G-d is totally above. He is above even having a name. He is just "You." Even before we say His name, we have an up-close and personal relationship with HaShem, You.
Ado-Nai	**G-d,** This is the true name of G-d. It is the way that G-d is, was and will always be. The four letters mark the flow of energy from the infinite to the finite.
Elo-Heinu	**Our G-d,** This name of G-d expresses the way that His power is felt in nature and in the world. And He is our G-d; we feel a personal connection to Him.
Melech ha'Olam	**King of the universe,** This is the way that He comes all the way down to be the king of the world. ***Olam—He'elem,*** but through this *brachah*, through our G-d given choice, we draw light into the *he'elem* (hiddenness) of the *olam*.
Shehakol niheyah bidvaro	***By whose word all things came to be.*** ***Devaro—His word—*** is the latent Divine Spark that now is released and revealed through this *brachah*.

Key Points

1. Our true self is not the body, but something beyond—the soul.

2. Every thing has its unique design or program which defines and controls that thing. In living creatures, we refer to that design as the "soul."

3. The uniquely human soul is metaphysical and eternal. It has the ability to comprehend abstract ideas and to think about G-d.

4. The human soul is a "spark" of G-d.

5. The soul is in the body to act as an interface between the spiritual and the physical. We are the translator between G-d and the world.

6. This is reflected in the unique way man was formed—first the body was formed from earth, and then the soul was blown into man from G-d's Essence. We combine the lowest and the highest—earth and a spark of G-d.

7. Every moment of life is an opportunity to elevate the world and experience G-dliness.

8. A *brachah* helps us become aware of these opportunities and take advantage of them.

Additional Readings

What is the Soul?

By **Rabbi Yanki Tauber**

Rabbon Gamliel's son, Shimon, would say: All my life I have been raised among the wise, and I have found nothing better for the body than silence . . . (Ethics of the Fathers, 1:17)

The Talmud goes even further, with the amazing statement: "What is man's task in the world? To make himself as silent as the dumb."[1] Obviously, one can think of many cases in which silence is advisable. But is there no greater virtue? And is this indeed the purpose of life?

Essentially, the world is words—divine words. "G-d said: 'Let there be light!' and there was light." G-d said: "May there be a firmament . . ." "May the waters gather . . ." "May the earth sprout forth . . . ,"[2] and our world, in all its infinite variety and complexity, came into being. As chassidic teaching explains, these divine utterances not only caused these creations to materialize; they were, and continue to be, the very stuff of their existence. What we experience as physical light is, in truth, G-d's articulation of His desire that there be light. Grass is our physical perception of the divine words "May the earth sprout forth greenery." And so on.

Obviously, what emanated from G-d's "mouth" was not a "voice" in any human or physical sense. The Torah uses terms from our experience so that by delving into their significance we can learn something of how G-d relates to our existence. In our case, the Torah wishes to describe an existence which, on the one hand, is distinct from its source, yet on the other, is utterly dependent upon it and possesses no reality other than that dependence. This is the significance of the metaphor "speech" in regard to creation.

When a person speaks, he creates something that extends beyond his own being. The thought that he had conceived, and which, up until now, has existed only within his mind, is now translated into words that

depart his person to attain an existence distinct from his. Nevertheless, they are utterly dependent upon him for existence: the moment he ceases to speak, the entity we refer to as his "speech" no longer exists. In other words, their existence can only be defined in terms of his ongoing involvement to create them.

So it is with the world. On the one hand, G-d desired that a world exist, that it constitute a reality that (at least in its own perception) is distinct from His. On the other hand, the world has no independent existence, possessing no reality other than G-d's constant involvement to create and sustain it. What model have we, in the human experience of reality, for such an entity? Speech. So what is the world? The closest we can come to answering this question in humanly comprehendible terms is to say: The world is G-d speaking.

There is, however, a single exception to this model for the essential nature of all created things: the soul of man. Every single creation is described by the Torah as having come into being by a divine utterance, except for the soul. The Zohar explains that the soul is not a divine word but a G-dly thought.

Referring to the above interpretation of the metaphor of speech, this means that the soul is a creation which does not "depart" from the all-pervading reality of G-d. A creation that not only senses its total dependence upon its source (as, deep down, every creation does), but one that does not even see itself as an "entity" distinct from its Creator.

Alone in a verbose world, the soul of man is a thing of silence. And its mission in life is to impart this silence to the world about it.[4]

This is an excerpt from *Beyond the Letter of the Law*, by Yanki Tauber, published by The Meaningful Life Center.

[1]. Talmud, Chulin 89a.
[2]. Genesis 1.
[3]. Zohar, part II, 119a; Ohr Torah (by Rabbi DovBer of

Mezeritch), 2c; Tanya, Chapter 2.

[4]. Based on an address by the Rebbe, Nissan 24, 5719 (May 2, 1959).

shine outward—out of our eyes, mouth and ears—a Temple with windows, not to let light in but to allow it to shine out. With your arms, your emotions, encircle the flame three times blessing the world, your family and yourself. Draw it in and let it shine out. Not just inspiration, but light.

The Candle of G-d

By **Ms. Neria Cohen**

"Ner Hashem nishmas adam"—"The soul of man is the candle of G-d." Proverbs 20:27

At the genesis of mankind, G-d breathed life into us, blowing from His innermost being into ours. With that breath—that divinely human life force—we are not meant to blow out candles, we are not meant to blow out souls, but to bless them.

It was the first birthday party that my not yet two-year-old niece, Galya, had ever attended. All the children gathered round the table and watched in excitement and awe as the candles on the birthday cake were lit.

"One, Two, Three," and everyone puffed out their cheeks ready to blow while Galya encircled the flames three times with her arms and covered her eyes to bless the candles as she does every Friday night. Galya looked up amazed and confused to find the others puffing and blowing as the flames danced and slanted trying in vain to cleave to the wick.

"NO BLOWING," says Galya's mother whenever she sneaks little blows at her Shabbos candles. Even though everyone else cheered at the blowing out of the candles, when Galya looked over at her mother smiling and beaming with pride, she knew that her not blowing, that her blessing, was a perfect moment for all time.

"The soul of man is the candle of G-d." Placed down here in this less than lit up world, our soul is meant to

Anorexia of the Soul

By **Dr. Ilsa J. Bick, MD**

"It hurts."

"How long?"

"Yesterday, and the day before that, and the day before that. Forever."

"What makes it better?"

"Exercise. Running, sit-ups. Can I do sit-ups?"

"No."

"Why?"

"You're in pain. You're starving."

"Oh, that. It wasn't so bad at first. And you're right, it hurts, and oh!" She writhes on the bed. "Oh, it's happening again! Do something!"

"Let me see."

She hesitates. Then, as gingerly as if she were releasing a newly hatched chick, she uncups her hands from her abdomen. She looks like an inmate from a concentration camp. Her abdomen is concave, gutted like a melon. Her ribs protrude; her limbs are as thin as dry twigs. A fine down coats her cheeks, because her brain thinks she's metamorphosing into a fetus. Moaning, she grits her teeth, pitted, brown and scarred from the acid that bathes them every time she vomits.

She is 12 or 40, blonde or brunette, white or black. She may be a he. Her decline has been gradual: a caprice, a diet to lose a few pounds. She's adept at pretense, at loading her plate with food and pushing it around. Then she dumps it, flushes it, gives it to the dog. Or she hides food under her bed, in shoes, above the acoustical tile of the hospital's ceiling. As her flesh melts away, she is drawn, as inexorably as a moth to a flame, to mirrors, to windows, to pools of water into which she will gaze at herself, noting this flaw and that. Eventually, she'll immolate herself. She'll eat herself up. And she has forgotten hunger. In the life of almost every anorectic, there comes a day when hunger has no meaning and the ability to know hunger vanishes.

I place the drum of my stethoscope on her belly. There's nothing, and then there's a faraway tinkle, and I see that she's nodding frantically to tell me that's it, that's when it hurts.

"You're having hunger pains."

"Hunger pains?"

"Yes. You're hungry. That's why you hurt. Your body knows it, but you have to listen. You need to eat." She acts as if I'm speaking Swahili. "Eat? Food?"

"Yes."

"Oh, no, you don't understand," she gnaws her chapped lips until they bleed, "I couldn't possibly do that."

———————————————

"It hurts." He bunches his fist over his heart. "Here. A long time. A year, maybe ten. Forever."

"Can you put a name to it?"

"You know the way a crow does when it's picking at a squirrel that's been run over? Like that. Stabbing."

"What makes it better?" The question confounds him. He looks out the window, as if the answer he seeks, so elusive, lies everywhere but within himself.

He is 15 or 50; he is white or black; his hair is blond, dark, streaked with gray; he wears an earring, or eschews jewelry. He's fit, or has a paunch. Like the anorectic, he may be a she. But let's call him a man, and let's say he's Jewish.

His life that he thought was going so well is not. Oh, he's successful. He's been accepted into a great college, is about to finish his Ph.D. He owns his own business, or thinks his boss is a jerk. He is married, cruising, divorced. His wife is wonderful, his girlfriend cheats, his lover is seeing someone else.

When he's not busy, there's an ache. But his ability to articulate why has deserted him. Like the anorectic, he believes he has willed his emotions into non-existence. Transforming his hunger into something else altogether, he suffers from a peculiar delusion: that he is self-contained, separate. But he still hurts. He suffers from a certain anorexia of the soul.

Finally, he speaks. "Better? I dunno. But when I see a beautiful painting . . . for a moment, I'm perfectly happy. And I want to paint."

"And then?" He grins ruefully. "Then I look at the next painting."

"Why don't you paint?"

"There's always something else, something . . . " He breaks off. I wait. He says, "When I was a kid, I used to walk by this synagogue. We didn't go, don't ask me why. Saturdays I went with Mom to the grocery store, and we'd walk by, and I remember people coming out, and the men talking, and the kids laughing, and the women together . . . "

It seems he needs to look everywhere else but at me. "I thought it'd be nice to be with them. That's when the pain would come, and I'd feel . . . "

"A hunger?"

"Yeah. Like wanting to paint. And the more I thought about it, the more it hurt." He clears his throat.

"Dumb. There's no point?"

"What do you mean?"

"The religion . . . . it's just something people make up to fill the void."

"An emptiness of the soul?"

"Yeah. Like sitting on a mountain, looking at a sunset. That feeling of awe . . . of, wow, how did it happen? That's where G-d comes in, why people pray. Because they know that they're small, that they'll die. But if they pray, they're part of something bigger. Maybe when they pray, they find that little piece of G-d inside. And the pain stops."

He halts, shocked by what he's said. The minutes pass. Then I ask, "What are you thinking?" He laughs without mirth. "Lunch. But I'm not hungry. But I thought about that merger, and this exhibition at the museum, and a new restaurant downtown. But the pain's not in my gut." Again, he puts his fist over his heart. "It's here. I'm empty, and I keep trying to fill myself up, but I can't."

"Do you try?"

"I do a lot."

Anyone can be busy, but are you fulfilled? You eschew nourishing your soul, but I'll bet you never forget to exercise, read the paper, watch the news, eat dinner, close that stock deal, have a drink, catch ER. Like your body, your soul needs its vitamins and, like your body, your soul probably won't realize how famished it really is until you listen to it and feed it. You want to paint, but you walk on. You see a synagogue, but you won't go in. You're amazed by the world and think there's G-d, but you can't pray, won't pray. Yet you're hungry. But rather than feed your soul, you lose yourself in planning your merger, where you'll have lunch, where you'll go this weekend. You'll do anything but allow yourself food.

"Why do you starve? You said the people in synagogue were happy. You're busy, but you're unhappy. Why won't you eat?"

"You mean," he fumbles a moment, "you mean, go?"

"Pick up a brush. Go. Learn."

He stares, as if I've lost my mind. "Go? Me? To synagogue?" He looks ready to leap from his chair. "Oh, no, you don't understand. I couldn't possibly do that."

Reprinted with permission from www.chabad.org

Lesson 2
Before You Were Born

Introduction

Where did you come from— not just yesterday or the days before, but before you were born? Was there nothing? It's hard to imagine not existing. Understanding your roots helps you understand who you are, and perhaps more importantly, who you can become.

Join us for Lesson Two of *Soul Quest,* where we will discover the origins of the soul, how life begins, and how you become you and gain your unique personality. We will also gain powerful insights into how to live life in line with your inner self.

Before You Were Born
Before You Were Born
Before You Were Born
Before You Were Born
Before You Were Born
Before You Were Born

Being and Becoming
Soul Formation

Text 1

כי הנשמה חלק אלו-ה ממעל

לקוטי תורה, בראשית

The soul is a part of G-d from above.

RABBI YITSCHAK LURIA, LIKUTEI TORAH, BEREISHIT/GENESIS

Text 2

אל-הי, נשמה שנתת בי טהורה היא

אתה בראתה, אתה יצרתה, אתה נפחת בי

ואתה משמרה בקרבי ואתה עתיד ליטלה ממני

ולהחזירה בי לעתיד לבוא

סידור נוסח האריז״ל, ברכות השחר

The soul that You have given within me is pure.

You have created it,

You have formed it,

You have breathed it into me,

And You preserve it within me.

SIDDUR, NUSACH HAARIZAL, MORNING PRAYERS

Four Worlds (Optional Section)

Table 2.1
Descent of the Soul into the Four Worlds

Words	World
[My G-d, the soul that] You have given within me	*Pre-World State*
Is pure.	*Atzilut*
You have created it,	*Beriah*
You have formed it,	*Yetzirah*
You have breathed it into me	*Asiyah*

Table 2.2
Five Dimensions of the Soul

Name	Translation	Concept
Yechidah	Singularity	Essence
Chayah	Life	Will
Neshamah	Soul	Thought/Mind
Ruach	Spirit	Speech/Emotion
Nefesh	Vitality	Action

Table 2.3
The Development of the Soul as It Descends

Words	World	Dimension of Soul
[My G-d, the soul that] You have given within me	*Pre-World State*	*Yechidah*
is pure.	*Atzilut*	*Chayah*
You have created it,	*Beriah*	*Neshamah*
You have formed it,	*Yetzirah*	*Ruach*
You have breathed it into me	*Asiyah*	*Nefesh*

Preparing for Dispatch

Deep Breathing

Text 3

ונפש השנית בישראל היא חלק אלוה ממעל ממש כמ״ש ״ויפח באפיו נשמת
חיים״ (בראשית ב,ז) ואתה נפחת בי וכמ״ש בזוהר מאן דנפח מתוכיה נפח פי׳
מתוכיותו ומפנימיותו שתוכיות ופנימיות החיות שבאדם מוציא בנפיחתו בכח

תניא פרק ב

"**A**nd He [G-d] breathed into his nostrils a soul of life (Bereishit 2:7) . . . ."
It is written in the *Zohar*, "He who blows, blows from within him," that is to say, from his inwardness and his innermost being. For it is of one's inward and innermost vitality that a person emits through blowing with force.

RABBI SHNE'UR ZALMAN OF LIADI, TANYA, CHAPTER 2

Rabbi Shne'ur Zalman of Liadi (1745–1812). Known as "the Alter Rebbe" and "the Rav"; Born in Liozna, Belarus; buried in Hadiach, Ukraine; chassidic Rebbe and founder of the Chabad movement; among the principal students of the Magid of Mezeritch. His numerous works include the *Tanya,* an early classic of Chassidism; *Torah Or* and *Likutei Torah*; and *Shulchan Aruch HaRav,* a rewritten code of Jewish law. He was succeeded by his son, Rabbi Dovber of Lubavitch.

Text 4 📜

והנה מודעת זאת מארז"ל שתכלית בריאת עולם הזה הוא שנתאוה הקב"ה
להיות לו דירה בתחתונים (תנחומא נשא טז). . . . שכך עלה ברצונו ית'
להיות נחת רוח לפניו ית' כד אתכפיא ס"א ואתהפך חשוכא לנהורא שיאיר
אור ה' אין סוף ב"ה במקום החשך והס"א של כל עוה"ז כולו ביתר שאת
ויתר עז ויתרון אור מן החשך מהארתו בעולמות עליונים

תניא פרק לו

> **T**he purpose for which this world was cre-
> ated is that G-d desired to have an abode
> in the lowest realm (Midrash Tanchuma,
> *Naso* 16)."

. . . . For such was His will—that He find it pleasurable when the negative is subjugated [to holiness], and
the darkness is transformed into [holy] light. This is in
order that in the place of the darkness and negative that
prevail throughout this world, the *Ein Sof* [light of G-d]
will shine forth with greater strength and intensity—
and with the superior quality of light that emerges from
the darkness—than its radiance in the higher worlds.

IBID., CHAPTER 36

Divine Ops

Text 5

It is imperative that every Jew know that he is an emissary of the Master of all, charged with the mission—wherever he may be—of bringing into reality G-d's will and intention in creating the universe, namely, to illuminate the world with the light of Torah and divine service. This is done through performing practical mitzvot and implanting in oneself fine character traits.

RABBI MENACHEM MENDEL SCHNEERSON, HAYOM YOM, 7 ADAR I

Rabbi Menachem Mendel Schneerson (1902–1994). Known as "the Lubavitcher Rebbe," or simply as "the Rebbe." Born in southern Ukraine. Rabbi Schneerson escaped from the Nazis, arriving in the US in June 1941. The towering Jewish leader of the twentieth century, the Rebbe inspired and guided the revival of traditional Judaism after the European devastation, and often emphasized that the performance of just one additional good deed could usher in the era of Mashiach.

Text 6

The soul's origin is a supernal pristine place. Afterwards, the soul descends through the progression of the worlds: "You have created it, You have formed it, You have breathed it into me," until it descends below and becomes invested in a body and the physical world. At this point, the purpose is to unite and connect the level of the soul the way it is below with the source of the soul above. The way to achieve this is for the soul to fulfill its mission through refining the body, the animate soul, and its portion in the world. Through this, one achieves the purpose of creation—to transform this lowest realm into a dwelling place for G-d.

RABBI YISRAEL BAAL SHEM TOV, KETER SHEM TOV, HOSAFOT, 424

Rabbi Yisrael ben Eliezer (1698–1760). Better known as the Baal Shem Tov or by the acronym Besht; rabbi and mystic; founder of the chassidic movement. Born in Okupy, Ukraine, he was orphaned as a child. The Baal Shem Tov served as a teacher and clay-digger, before founding the chassidic movement. Although he never committed his ideas to writing, the Baal Shem Tov's teachings were gathered by his disciples in various volumes.

Mission Assignment

Text 7

Rabbi Yehudah Aryeh Leib Alter (1847–1905). Rabbi, chassidic master, and author. At age 23 he assumed the leadership of the chassidic dynasty of Ger (Gora), a town near Warsaw, Poland. His grandfather was Rabbi Yitschak Meir of Ger, the founder of the Ger dynasty and its first leader. He is commonly referred to as the Sfat Emet, after the title of his chassidic work on the Torah and commentary to the Talmud.

The Mishnah teaches that every Jew has a portion in the world to come. This is not stated in the future tense, rather, in the present. He has this portion now . . . . Each and every activity contains this very "portion," which is hidden within the physical activity.

RABBI YEHUDAH ARYEH LEIB ALTER,
SEFAT EMET, TAZRIA 5631; ACHAREI 5657

Learning Activity 1

Viktor Frankl writes that one who knows the "why" for his existence will be able to bear almost any "how." Take a moment to identify your spiritual mission. Is there a mitzvah you are passionate about? Conversely, is there a mitzvah that you struggle with? Or is there a mitzvah that only you can do? Take a moment to identify a particular mission that is your "portion in the world."

Basic Training

Text 8a 📖

דרש רבי שמלאי: למה הולד דומה במעי אמו? . . . ונר דלוק לו על ראשו

וצופה ומביט מסוף העולם ועד סופו,

שנאמר (איוב כט,ג) "בהלו נרו עלי ראשי לאורו אלך חשך"

תלמוד בבלי נדה ל,ב

Rabbi Simlai delivered the following discourse:
What does a fetus resemble when it is inside
its mother?

. . . . A light burns above its head and it looks and sees
from one end of the world to the other, as it is said,
"Then his lamp shined above my head, and by His light
I walked through darkness (Iyov/Job 29:3)."

TALMUD, NIDAH 30B

Text 8b 📖

Prior to birth it is shown the entire creation
within the context of its Divine purpose. The
soul is shown that all that G-d created, He created for His glory. Even though this glory is not apparent,
through the light of the candle, it is shown that there is
no place in the world where this glory does not exist.

BASED ON RABBI TSADOK HAKOHEN, PRI TSADIK, NOACH 5

Rabbi Tsadok HaCohen Rabinowitz of Lublin (1823–1900). Chassidic Rebbe and prolific author of works on Chassidism. Born into a Lithuanian rabbinic family, he became a follower of Rabbi Mordechai Yosef Leiner of Izbica as a young man. After the passing of his colleague, Rabbi Leibel Eiger, he became Rebbe in Lublin. He authored many works on Jewish law, Chassidism, Kabbalah, and ethics, as well as scholarly essays on astronomy, geometry, and algebra. He is buried in Lublin.

Text 9a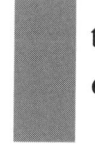

ומלמדין אותו כל התורה כולה

תלמוד בבלי נדה ל,ב

It is also taught all the Torah from beginning to end.

TALMUD, NIDAH 30B, OP. CIT.

Text 9b

Rabbi Shimon bar Yochai (2nd century CE). Known by the acronym Rashbi; scholar of the Mishnah and founder of Jewish mysticism; an eminent disciple of Rabbi Akiva. The kabbalistic classic *Sefer HaZohar* is attributed to him and his disciples. Because of the Roman persecutions he was forced to hide with his son Eliezer for 13 years. Lag Ba'Omer is commemorated as the day of his passing, with thousands visiting his grave in Meron, Israel.

קודשא בריך הוא אסתכל באורייתא וברא עלמא
בר נש מסתכל בה באורייתא ומקיים עלמא

זוהר ב קסא,ב

The Holy One, blessed be He, looked into the Torah and created the world; man looks into the Torah and keeps the world in existence.

RABBI SHIMON BAR YOCHAI, ZOHAR II,161B

The Pledge

Text 10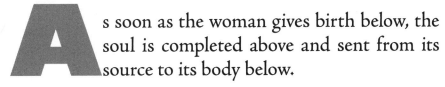

ואינו יוצא משם עד שמשביעין אותו . . . ומה היא השבועה שמשביעין אותו?
תהי צדיק ואל תהי רשע

תלמוד בבלי נדה ל,ב

I t does not emerge from there before it is made to take an oath . . . . What is the nature of the oath that it is made to take? Be righteous and do not be wicked.

TALMUD, NIDAH 30B, OP. CIT.

Soul Escalator (Going Down!)
Birth

Text 11

A s soon as the woman gives birth below, the soul is completed above and sent from its source to its body below.

RABBI AVIGDOR BEN YITSCHAK KARA, SEFER HAPELIAH

Rabbi Avigdor ben Yitschak Kara (d. 1439). Rabbinical judge of Prague; kabbalist, philosopher, and liturgical poet. He enjoyed a high reputation with King Wenceslaus, who liked to converse with him on religious matters. After surviving a pogrom in 1389 that killed 3000 Jews, he composed a famous liturgical eulogy. Some of his works try to synthesize Kabbalah and philosophy. Some attribute the kabbalistic works *Sefer HaKanah* and *Sefer HaPeliah* to him.

Rabbi Shlomo ben Yitschak (Yitschaki) (1040–1105). Better known by the acronym *Rashi*; Rabbi and famed author of the first comprehensive commentaries on the Talmud and Bible. Born in Troyes, Champagne, Rashi studied in the famed *yeshivot* of Mainz and Worms. His commentaries, which focus on the simple understanding of the text, are considered fundamental to Torah study. Since their initial printings, they have appeared in virtually every edition of the Talmud and Bible. Many of the famed Tosafists of France are among Rashi's descendants.

Text 12

דכל זמן שלא יצא לאויר העולם לאו נפש הוא

רש"י סנהדרין עב,ב

As long as the child is not yet born, it is not a *nefesh* [an independent living entity].

RASHI, SANHEDRIN 72B

And Beyond

Text 13

The entry of the holy soul begins with the process of education in Torah and mitzvah performance as required by the Sages. [For males, it begins] also through the mitzvah of *milah*—circumcision.

RABBI SHNE'UR ZALMAN OF LIADI,
CODE OF JEWISH LAW, MAHADURA TIN'YANA, ORACH CHAIM, 4:2

Text 14

תא חזי בר נש דאתיליד לא אתמנא עליה חילא דלעילא עד דאתגזר כיון
דאתגזר אתער עליה אתערותא דרוחא דלעילא, זכי לאתעסקא באורייתא
אתער עליה אתערותא יתיר, זכי ועביד פקודי אורייתא, אתער עליה אתערותא
יתיר, זכי ואתנסיב זכי ואוליד בנין ואוליף לון ארחוי דמלכא קדישא הא כדין
הוא אדם שלים

זוהר ג צא,ב

bserve that when a male child is born, a power from above is not appointed to watch over him until he is circumcised. When a male child is circumcised, some supernal activity is stirred in connection with it. If he proceeds to the study of the Torah, the activity is heightened. If he is able to keep the precepts of the Law, the activity is still further heightened. If he advances so far as to marry and beget children and teach them the ways of the Holy King, then he is a complete man.

ZOHAR, OP. CIT., III, 91B

Learning Activity 2

Birthdays mark the flowering of new perspectives and powers for approaching life. Can you identify some new spiritual milestone that you have achieved in the last year?

Key Points

1. The essence of the soul is its G-dliness.

2. This essence must undergo many stages and changes in order to fuse with the body, creating many "layers" within the soul.

3. Souls are "born" in order to serve as Divine Operatives and complete a mission.

4. Every soul has a unique mission and portion of the world to elevate.

5. Anything done as part of the Divine mission becomes part of the soul's eternal existence.

6. The soul is taught the entire Torah and administered an oath to aid it in fulfilling its mission.

7. Life's milestones mark new stages in the unfolding of the mission, and new opportunities to expand our true being.

Additional Readings

Birth: The Mission Begins

By **Rabbi Simon Jacobson**

You are my child, I have given birth to you today.
Psalms, 2:7

Birth is G-d saying you matter.
The Rebbe

At a gathering of family and friends celebrating a child's birth, the Rebbe explained the three reasons to rejoice at such an occasion: the joy of the entire nation for the birth of a new member, the joy of the parents for being blessed with a child, and the joy of the child for having been brought into the world. "But how can we celebrate when we don't yet know how a child will turn out?" one man asked. "Birth marks the moment when the soul enters the body," said the Rebbe. "And because the soul is connected directly to G-d, that is reason enough to rejoice."

Why Were You Born?

What your birth means is that you are G-d's child. Your birth was not an accident; G-d chooses each of us to fulfill a specific mission in this world, just as a composer lovingly arranges each musical note. Take away even one note, and the composition falls apart. Each person matters; each person is irreplaceable. Your life is always leading you toward your destiny, and every single moment is meaningful and precious.

Many people seem to feel that, just because we didn't *choose* to enter the world, our birth is a stroke of coincidence or serendipity. This couldn't be further from the truth. Birth is G-d's way of saying that He has invested His will and energy in creating you; G-d feels great joy when you are born, the greatest pleasure imaginable, for the moment of birth encompasses the potential for all future achievements.

When, Exactly Does Life Begin?

At birth, the soul enters the body, creating a life that sustains itself, an autonomous human being. A fetus, of course, is a living organism complete with functioning brain, heart, and limbs. But it is only an extension, albeit a living one, of its mother's being. It *contains* life but is not yet an independent life, sustained by its own force.

So the moment of birth marks the beginning of our mission on earth, which is to transform our material world into a vehicle of spiritual expression and G-dliness. The life process is much more than simple biology. It is about growth, development, and fulfilling our potential. A person is not fully alive unless he is attuned to his soul's higher purpose, unless he realizes its mission.

Many of us *sense* a spiritual side to our lives. Perhaps we even seek it out at times. But because we are so busy with our daily lives and so hungry for instant gratification, we forget—or never take the time to learn—why we are here in the first place.

Each of us has a choice: We can be merely biologically alive or we can be truly alive, *spiritually* alive. Even as adults, we can live the way a fetus does—eating, drinking, and sleeping, a complete person that is missing its most vital element: a soul. Or we can take advantage of our capacity to be spiritually sensitive, and participate in the world.

It is tempting to spend our lives in a fetus-like state. Even the sages admit this: "It is more pleasant not to be born than to be born." Wouldn't it be easier to go through life warm and well fed, protected from the outside world, than to endure the harsh forces of life we have all come to know?

Indeed, many of us *do* try to insulate ourselves, reacting to life but never fully engaging it. In this light, we see that birth, above all else, is a *challenge*, the first and perhaps most difficult challenge we will ever face.

For a moment, think about the experiences of an infant. Now try to picture your own birth. What a monumental moment that was! What feelings did you have? What voices did you hear? Scientists and psychologists are only beginning to acknowledge what the Torah has been teaching for thousands of years: that our experiences as a newborn baby have a profound impact on our inner psyches. A newborn is as receptive as a dry sponge. He hears perhaps even more than an adult hears; precisely *because* his conscious mind is not yet at work, and *because* he doesn't understand the words, a newborn is much more impressionable. He absorbs everything in his environment in the purest form, unadulterated by the adult ego or intellect.

Education, therefore, begins the moment a child is born. This presents us with a profound responsibility as to how we behave in the presence of a child, and how we treat children from the moment of birth. Remember: the soul of a newborn child is fully alive, with open ears that hear everything.

A revered rabbi, when he was an infant, was often carried in his bassinet to hear prayers and songs. He grew up to be a great scholar, and, in acknowledgment of how he was raised, he was often greeted with the blessing, "Beloved is the one who gave birth to you."

This is an excerpt from *Toward a Meaningful Life—The Wisdom of the Rebbe,* by Rabbi Simon Jacobson.

Me and My Body: a Dialogue

By **Rabbi Tzvi Freeman**

For generations, the body was looked upon as the evil perpetrator and seductress. The only way to deal with it was with a big stick, hurting it and starving it with the hope that it would eventually surrender to the soul. Then along came the Baal Shem Tov and taught that we can work *with* the body rather than against it.

"When you will see the donkey of your enemy crouching under its load . . . " (Exodus 23:5).

You thought that's talking about a beast of burden, teaching us a lesson in compassion for animals. Well it is. But the Baal Shem Tov saw it as also speaking of another kind of animal, one even closer to home: Your body.

Your body is crouching under its load, because it doesn't get this whole spirituality trip. The soul loaded it up with its own soulful baggage and told it to move, but it doesn't feel particularly cut out for the job. The soul wants wisdom, the body wants potato chips. The soul is drawn to be absorbed within the Infinite Light, the body is drawn to be absorbed into its pillow.

And so, the body becomes your enemy's donkey— collaborating with the dark side to foil, subterfuge, frustrate and exasperate every gambit of the soul for spiritual freedom.

You want to fast and beat it up. "Stop crouching!" you want to scream. "Get up and carry that load!" That's what spiritual seekers used to do. Before the Baal Shem Tov.

But the Baal Shem Tov pointed out that's not what the rest of the verse says to do: "When you will see the donkey of your enemy crouching under its load, and you want to abandon it there, don't abandon it. Help it out."

"Get it on your side," the Baal Shem Tov taught. "Make it a partner in your spiritual quest."

What changed?

Really the Baal Shem Tov had to say this. The Baal Shem Tov was a man so obsessed with G-dliness, he saw it everywhere he looked. "G-dliness is everything and everything is G-dliness," he declared. "G-d supervises each event," the Baal Shem Tov taught, "because He is found within each event. Because without Him there, nothing exists. The truth of all things is nothing more than His breath and His light."

Because he was an extremist about G-dliness, the Baal Shem Tov had to be tolerant with the body. Since the ultimate truth is that there is nothing else—no entity or event outside of the Infinite Light—that has to include the meat patty you're living inside called a body. So if your journey leaves the body behind, then it's not G-dliness you're traveling towards. If the body's needs and demands contradict your spiritual path, then that path is not taking you to the ultimate truth.

If so, why is the body forever getting in the way of every advance of the soul upward? My personal explanation is that the body simply has a problem with its self-esteem.

Let's say we would ask the body. What would it answer? You turn to your crouching donkey and you say:

Soul: "Donkey! You're crouching again! Get up! I need to meditate and pray so I can achieve mystic union with the Infinite Light."

Body: "Don't wanna get up."

S: So what do you want?

B: Want potato chips. Salt & Vinegar kind. With salsa dip.

S: Is that all?

B: No. Is there a Jacuzzi somewhere around here?

S: I'm talking about the ultimate ecstasy of bonding with the Infinite, and all you can think of is eating chips in a hot tub? I think what you need is another good cleansing fast!"

B: Don't even think of trying.

S: Oh yeah? Why not?

B: Cuz what happened last time?

S: Uh, I got a headache and couldn't meditate, so I quit.

B: You try that again and I'll give you a whopper headache this time like you never had before.

S: You are nasty! So I'm gonna stay up tonight learning Zohar until dawn, then I'll pray with the sunrise, then . . .

B: Then you'll catch a lousy virus and be stuck in bed for a week. Great place for your spiritual quest there, right?

S: Okay, a little Zohar every night.

B: Not interested.

S: Twice a week?

B: You wanna do that, I'm gonna put some heavy demands on you.

S: Like what.

B: Hey, buddy, chips and Jacuzzis are child's play. You wanna play with the big boys—we're on!

S: No! Please! Why are you doing this to me? Why are you imprisoning me like this?

B: Because you are the enemy.

S: Enemy? Don't I feed you daily? Find you a nice bed at night, lead you safely through the dark valleys of life . . .

B: Sure. But you don't give me what I really want.

S: What do you really want? Steak every night?

B: Naaah. Can do without.

S: Unlimited TV time?

B: Dull. Nothing there these days.

S: A lifetime supply of potato chips?

B: You kidding? All that sodium could kill a human body.

S: SO IF YOU DON'T NEED THESE THINGS, WHY DO YOU KEEP DEMANDING THEM FROM ME EVERY TIME I WANT TO GO HIGHER!!??

B: BECAUSE YOU KEEP IGNORING ME LIKE I DON'T EXIST!!!

S: [silent]

S: [still silent]

B: Look, I'm sorry I yelled, but you have to understand. Life with you makes me feel so darned worthless. Next to you, I'm really nothing.

S: You really feel that way?

B: How could anybody not feel totally worthless being married to a G-dly being whose only interest is complete re-absorption within higher and yet higher planes of light—while I sit here like a millstone around your neck, just reminding you once in a while that we have to go to the washroom?

S: Well, I never really looked at it that way.

B: You don't look at it that way. About everything else and everyone else you're so altruistic. You're ready to sacrifice your very being for the sake of G-d's perfect oneness. But when it comes to me, to your own body, you just have no clue.

S: I had no clue . . .

B: Listen, you think I'm a dumb hamburger with eyeballs, right? You think I'm filled with self-serving, egoistic, narcissistic stuffings, a real me-bag. But the truth is, I know the truth better than you do. I know I'm absolutely nothing, of no worth, not even of any substance before the reality of the Infinite Light you relate to so well.

S: So if you know the truth, why do you fight against it?

B: And just be nothing?

S: Yeah!

B: Cuz I don't want to be nothing! I want to be something! A real something—not just cuz some idiot in the yoga class says hey that's some real flex you got there, or some dork at the ashram is so impressed at how long I can sit in full lotus without wetting my khakis . . . that's just more stupid nothin' games and I know it!

S: So what kind of something do you want to be?

B: The only real something I know how to be.

S: Which is?

B: Which is when you realize that I am a force to be reckoned with!

S: Why me?

B: Cuz I know that you are the one thing in this world that is for real, and if you have to reckon with me, hey that makes me real too! Right?

S: [silent]

B: [also silent]

S: Hey, body, I have to tell you something.

B: Not interested.

S: It's a story. A personal story.

B: Then it needs potato chips. And violence and romance.

S: It has all of that. You see, before I came here, I was in the highest place in the universe. It's called The Garden of Eden, and it goes higher and higher, and I was like at level 3100 and moving up. There, you don't have TV. You got way better. You get to bask in rays of light from the Shechinah, in perfect bliss and ecstasy, as that light constantly increases its intensity as you increase your capacity to absorb.

B: What's to eat?

S: Eat? Heck, souls stand in line for years to get to these places. There's no restaurant, entertainment or amusement park anywhere close to this in the galaxy. Returning souls are willing to suffer the fires of gehenna for years just to get a back seat to the show. I'm telling you, a lifetime of every pleasure this world has to offer doesn't come close to one moment of the delight of that world.

B: So how on earth did you end up down here then?

S: That's where the violence comes in.

B: I'm listening.

S: I was violently ripped away from my true place above in that Divine Light—and thrown down here below to be imprisoned within . . .

B: . . . yours truly. Thanks allot. Listen, if you didn't want to be here, you didn't have to consent.

S: I was forced. Against my will.

B: But admit it, you were interested, right? Otherwise . . .

S: Sure I was interested . . .

B: For the chips, right?

S: You mean the gambling chips?

B: That too.

S: Sure.

B: Sure . . .

S: No really. I knew it was a gamble, but I figured, hey maybe there's a chance.

B: A chance of what?

S: A chance to get even higher. So I took the gamble.

B: Gamble on what?

S: Gamble on you.

B: Me? What kind of a dumb investment is that?

S: The ultimate investment! Look, there I was going higher . . .

B: . . . and higher without end. Yeah we got that part already. Been there . . .

S: . . . done that. So I said, I gotta get beyond this. I gotta get to the Source. The Source where all this light is coming from. The Real Essence.

B: Wuzzat?

S: He Himself. Not just Garden of Eden. Not just light. Not even the Infinite Light. The Absolute.

B: Kewel. So how d'ya get it?

S: Well, I figured I can't get it on my own, because, you see, I'm a being of light. Wherever I go, wherever I look, there's just light. No real being-ness. No real sense of "hey, I am here." To get to the Absolute, the core and essence, I need to invest in something that has that drive, that need to be something, that sense of "I"—cuz, how can you experience the ultimate true I, if you don't have an I yourself?

B: So where do you get that?

S: In you.

B: In who?

S: I said you.

B: You said me?

S: Right.

B: [silent]

B: Oh my . . . You mean I am the key to your ultimate experience?

S: Well actually . . .

B: Actually, my ultimate experience too.

S: Perhaps yours even more than mine. The way it works is that if I can turn you for a moment away from the TV and the chips and all that big boy stuff too and just once get you really involved in a down-to-earth, shiny and beautiful mitzvah . . .

B: Then you get . . .

S: Then, at that point in time, we both get The Essence. The Ultimate. He Himself. And then it's all worth it. Way worth it.

B: Kewel. I'm in.

S: It's a deal.

B: So where do I get these mitzvah thingies?

S: Well we can start by putting you on a kosher diet.

B: I can do a diet, as long as . . .

S: Sure, we got kosher potato chips. Then there's Shabbat, when you have to enjoy all the foods you really like. Then . . .

B: I love you, soul.

S: I told you there would be romance.

"In the Time To Come," wrote the Rebbe Maharash (Rabbi Shmuel of Lubavitch, 1834–1882), "the soul will be nurtured by the body. Because in truth, the body comes from a place immeasurably higher than the soul."

Reprinted with permission from www.chabad.org

Soul Awakenings

By **Rabbi Shaul Yosef Leiter**

Translated and adapted from Meah Shearim and other sources

My G-d, the soul which You have placed within me is pure. You have created it, You have formed it, You have breathed it into me, and You preserve it within me. You will eventually take it from me, and restore it within me in Time to Come. So long as the soul is within me, I offer thanks to You, L-rd my G-d and G-d of my fathers, Master of all works, L-rd of all souls. Blessed are You L-rd, who restores souls to dead bodies. (Liturgy, Morning Blessings)

Eighteen morning blessings are said each day upon arising, after one has dressed and washed hands. This, the third blessing, deals with the Jewish soul.

"A person is a small world" (*Bereishit Rabba* 78:12). In a sense each one of us reflects the entire creation. While we are asleep, conscious control is suspended and our souls return to their source. This corresponds to the state of reality before the world was created. When a person awakens and his divine soul reenters his body, he re-enacts the creation by drawing the divine energy back into him.

My G-d . . . Who is talking here? Given that a human being is an entity comprised of different spiritual and physical elements, the speaker cannot be the body, for the body without the soul is like an inanimate rock.

. . . the soul . . . On the other hand, if the speaker is the soul, why is it referring to itself in third person?

. . . which You have placed . . . The basis for the answer is that in addition to his body, every Jew has two souls - a *G-dly soul* that is linked to the Infinite, and an *animal* (animating, animalistic) *soul*, totally bound by material reality. The G-dly soul is derived from G-d's essence (see Tanya I, ch. 2); this is what is meant by "the soul which *You* have given."

. . . within me . . . Just as the animal soul is clothed within the body (its intellect in the brain, its emotions in the heart, and so on) and through it, seeks to fulfill its desires, so too the G-dly soul finds expression by being clothed within the animal soul. The speaker here is the animal soul, making a statement about the G-dly soul within it. "Within me" hints that while this condition is a benefit for the animating soul, it nevertheless constitutes a state of exile for the divine soul.

The descent of the divine soul through the Four Worlds (stages or spiritual dimensions in the process of Creation) is now described:

. . . is pure. It originates in the world of Emanation, known as *Atzilut*.

You have created it. It descends through the world of Creation, or *Beriya*. Note that the Hebrew word for "created it", "*barata*", in the blessing literally uses the same term as the supernal world associated with it.

You have formed it. This comes from the world of Formation, or *Yetzira*. Note that the Hebrew word for "formed it", "*yetzarta*", in the blessing uses the same term as the supernal world associated with it.

You have breathed it . . . from the world of Action, or *Asiya* . . .

. . . into me . . . . into this physical world.

You preserve it within me . . . The soul longs to leave the confines of the body and return to its previous level, like a flame that naturally ascends, as it is taught (*Avot* 4), "Against your will, you live." Furthermore, you guard it from doing evil within me, as it is written, "If G-d did not aid the soul in its task, it would be unable to overcome the evil inclination" (*Kiddushin* 30b).

And in the future you will take it from me . . . The primary purpose of the soul's descent into the body is to gain the merit to eventually cling to G-d on an even higher level than it did previously. The soul attains this merit by influencing the rest of the animal soul of the body to conduct itself properly.

. . . and return it within me in Time to Come. G-d will restore the soul as well as the body at the time of the Revival of the Dead.

So long as the soul is within me . . . In the morning, one's soul is refreshed and, more than at any other time, is free from evil thoughts and impulses. He feels pure. What better time is there for the animal soul to thank the Creator for His gift of potential growth?

I offer thanks to You, my G-d and G-d of my fathers, Master of all works . . . Ultimately even the animal soul realized that its existence, too, is dependent on G-d.

L-rd of all souls . . . It is to You we will have to answer. "L-rd", in Hebrew "*Adon*", refers to the divine name associated with justice, *Ado-nai*.

Blessed are You, G-d, who returns souls to dead bodies. Sleep approximates a 60th part of death (*Berachot* 57b). The animal soul simultaneously affirms the new opportunity for the day and expresses faith in the future Revival of the Dead.

Lesson 3
Death and Beyond

Introduction

Where does the soul go after leaving this world? Where are my departed loved ones? What is it like in heaven? The afterlife has been one of the most mysterious and alluring enigmas to man since the day Adam set foot on earth.

In Lesson Three of *Soul Quest,* we explore the deep mysteries of death and the afterlife. Trace the soul's path as it departs this world, and see how understanding the destination can make your journey more meaningful.

Death and Beyond

Death and Departure
Transitions

Rabbi Shimon bar Yochai (2nd century CE). Known by the acronym Rashbi; scholar of the Mishnah and founder of Jewish mysticism; an eminent disciple of Rabbi Akiva. The kabbalistic classic *Sefer HaZohar* is attributed to him and his disciples. Because of the Roman persecutions he was forced to hide with his son Eliezer for 13 years. Lag Ba'Omer is commemorated as the day of his passing, with thousands visiting his grave in Meron, Israel.

Text 1

ולית לה לנפשא קשיו בכלא כפרישו דילה מן גופא

זוהר ג פח,א

othing is as hard for the soul as its separation from the body.

RABBI SHIMON BAR YOCHAI, ZOHAR III, 88A

Text 2

תא חזי בשעתא דבר נש קאים למיהך לההוא עלמא והוא בבי מרעיה אתיין עליה ג׳ שלוחין וחמי תמן מה דלא יכיל בר נש למחמי כד איהו בהאי עלמא, וההוא יומא יומא דדינא עלאה הוא דמלכא בעי פקדונא דיליה, זכאה ההוא בר נש דפקדוניה אתיב למלכא כמה דאתיהיב ליה בגויה

זוהר ג פח,א

bserve that when a man is on his deathbed and at the point of departing for the other world, three messengers are sent to him, and he sees what other men cannot see in this world. That day is a day of heavenly judgment on which the King demands back his deposit. Happy is the man who can restore the deposit just as it was given to him.

IBID.

Text 3 🕮

בההוא זמנא דמטא שעתא לאתפרשא לא נפקא נפשא מן גופא עד
דאתגלי עליה שכינתא ונפשא מגו חדותא וחביבותא דשכינתא נפקא
מגופא לקבלהא, אי זכאה הוא מתקשר בה ואתדבק בה, ואי לאו שכינתא
אזלא והיא אשתארת ואזלת ומתאבלת על פרישותא דגופא

זוהר ג נג,א

When the moment arrives for the soul to depart from the body, [the soul] does not actually leave until the *Shechinah* shows itself to it. If [the person] is righteous, [the soul] cleaves and attaches itself to [the *Shechinah*]. But if not, the *Shechinah* departs, and the soul is left behind, mourning for its separation from the body.

ZOHAR III, OP. CIT., 53A

Text 4 🕮

העולם הזה דומה לפרוזדור לפני העולם הבא
התקן עצמך בפרוזדור כדי שתכנס לטרקלין

משנה אבות ד,טז

This world is like the vestibule of the world to come. Prepare yourself in the vestibule so that you may enter the banquet hall.

MISHNAH, AVOT 4:16

Four Levels of Separation

Text 5a

כל תלתא יומין נפשא טייסא על גופא סבירה דהיא חזרה לגביה
כיון דהיא חמייא דאישתני זיויהון דאפוי היא שבקא ליה ואזלה לה

תלמוד ירושלמי מועד קטן ג,ה

For three days, the soul hovers above the body, considering whether to return. After three days, when it sees that the face has changed, it leaves the body and departs.

JERUSALEM TALMUD, MOED KATAN 3:5

Text 5b

כל ז׳ יומין נשמתא אזלא מביתיה לקבריה ומקבריה לביתיה ואתאבלת
עלוי דגופא . . . בתר ז׳ יומין גופא הוי כמה דהוה ונשמתיה עאלת לדוכתא

זוהר א ריח,ב

All seven days [of mourning], the soul leaves the house and goes to the grave, and from the grave to the house, and mourns the body . . . . After seven days . . . it goes on its way to its place.

ZOHAR, OP. CIT., I, 218B

Text 5c

כל אינון תלתין יומין אתדנו נפשא וגופא כחדא, ובגיני כך אשתכח נשמתא
לתתא בארעא . . . לבתר נשמתא סלקא וגופא אתבלי בארעא

זוהר ב קצט,ב

All those thirty days, the soul and the body are judged as one, and thus the soul is found below . . . after that, the soul departs and the body erodes in the earth.

ZOHAR, OP. CIT., II, 199B

Text 5d

כל שנים עשר חדש גופו קיים, ונשמתו עולה ויורדת
לאחר שנים עשר חדש הגוף בטל, ונשמתו עולה, ושוב אינה יורדת

תלמוד בבלי שבת קנב,ב

For twelve months, the body exists and the soul ascends and descends; after twelve months, the body becomes null and the soul rises and does not return.

TALMUD, SHABBAT 152B

Soul Catharsis

Learning Activity 1

What is the benefit of letting children feel the consequences of their behavior?

Take two minutes to come up with as many benefits as you can.

Text **6**

כדין נחתין עליה תלת שליחן מנן, חד דכתיב כל זכוון וכל חובין דעבד בר נש בהאי עלמא, וחד דעביד חושבן יומוי, וחד דהוה אזיל עמיה כד הוה במעי אמיה
זוהר ב קצט,א

Then three appointed messengers descend upon the man: one of them makes a record of all the good deeds and the misdeeds that he has performed in this world; one casts up the reckoning of his days; and the third is the one who has accompanied the man from the time when he was in his mother's womb.

ZOHAR, OP. CIT., II, 199A

Text 7 📜

נשמתין כד סלקין אסתחיין בההוא נהר די נור וסלקין לקורבנא
ולא אתוקדן אלא אסתחיין . . . נשמתא די נור דאתנטילת מגו
כורסייא קדישא דכתיב בה ״כרסיה שביבין די נור״, בזמנא דבעיא
לאסתחיא מההוא זוהמא דבה אתעברת בנורא ואסתחיא, ונורא
אכלא כל ההוא זוהמא די בנשמתא, ונשמתא אסתחיא ואתלבנת
זוהר ב ריא,ב

The souls of people, before ascending into
Paradise, are immersed in that "river of fire" . . .
where they are purged without being consumed
. . . . The soul originated in fire, coming from beneath
the throne of glory which is of fire . . . . Thus, fire alone
has the virtue of consuming every pollution of the soul
and making the soul emerge pure and white.

ZOHAR, OP. CIT., II, 211B

Absolute Paradise

True Delight

Text 8 📜

For twelve months [after death], the power of the
body still exists, and the soul is inclined to the
body's knowledge and deeds with physical images,
as it was accustomed to during physical life . . . . After

twelve months, it transcends the ideas of the physical [realm], wears a cloak of royalty, and is coronated with the crown of *Gan Eden* (Paradise).

Gan Eden is the gate to heaven, where one experiences the light of life . . . . And through the comprehension of the soul of that place, it ascends, to become attached to a higher supernal realm and delights of spiritual understanding . . . .

Ramban (Nachmanides), Sha'ar HaGemul

Text 9a

דע כי כשם שלא ישיג הסומא את הצבעים, ולא ישיג החרש את הקולות, . . . כך לא ישיגו הגופות התענוגות הנפשיים . . . לא יודע בעולם הזה הגשמי תענוגי העולם הרוחני, לפי שאין אצלינו כלל עונג זולת עונג הגופות בלבד . . . ולא נכירהו ולא נשיגהו בעיון ראשון אלא אחרי חקירה מרובה

פירוש המשנה להרמב"ם סנהדרין, פרק י, הקדמה

Just as a blind man cannot comprehend color and the deaf cannot comprehend sound . . . so too, the body cannot comprehend delights of the soul . . . in this physical world we cannot know the spiritual world . . . we can only come to know it through much inquiry.

Rambam (Maimonides), Commentary on Mishnah, Introduction to Sanhedrin, Chapter 10

Text 9b 📖

 והוא העולם הבא שבו תשכיל נפשינו מן הבורא בדומה למה שמשכילים
הגרמים העליונים או יותר, הרי אותו התענוג לא יתחלק ולא יתואר ואין
למצוא משל להמשיל בו אותו התענוג

פירוש המשנה להרמב״ם סנהדרין, פרק י, הקדמה

In the world to come, our souls will understand the knowledge of the Creator, blessed be He, as the supernal bodies comprehend Him. The pleasure derived from this is not split into parts, and cannot be told, nor can any parable be found to explain this delight.

Ibid.

Feel the One

Text 10 📖

יפה שעה אחת בתשובה ומעשים טובים בעולם הזה מכל חיי העולם הבא
ויפה שעה אחת של קורת רוח בעולם הבא מכל חיי העולם הזה

משנה אבות ד,יז

Better is one hour of repentance and good deeds in this world than the whole life of the world to come; and better is one hour of bliss in the world to come than the whole life of this world.

Mishnah, Avot 4:17

Figure **3.1**

Pleasure of one hour in the world to come **>** all the pleasure of this world
Value of one hour of good deeds in this world **>** the value of all of the world to come

Text **11** 📜

Rabbi Shne'ur Zalman of Liadi (1745–1812). Known as "the Alter Rebbe" and "the Rav"; Born in Liozna, Belarus; buried in Hadiach, Ukraine; chassidic Rebbe and founder of the Chabad movement; among the principal students of the Magid of Mezeritch. His numerous works include the *Tanya,* an early classic of Chassidism; *Torah Or* and *Likutei Torah*; and *Shulchan Aruch HaRav,* a rewritten code of Jewish law. He was succeeded by his son, Rabbi Dovber of Lubavitch.

שאויר ג"ע מתפשט סביב כל אדם ונרשמים באויר זה כל מחשבותיו
ודבוריו הטובים בתורה ועבודת ה' (וכן להיפך ח"ו נרשמים באויר
המתפשט מגיהנם סביב כל אדם)

תניא, אגרת הקודש כז

The atmosphere of the *Gan Eden* envelops every individual, and in this atmosphere are recorded all of one's good thoughts and utterances of Torah and divine worship; and likewise to the contrary, heaven forfend: [negative thoughts and utterances] are recorded in the atmosphere from Gehenna which envelops every individual.

RABBI SHNE'UR ZALMAN OF LIADI, TANYA, IGERET HAKODESH 27B

Text **12** 📜

ששכר מצוה מצוה

משנה אבות ד,ב

The reward for a mitzvah is a mitzvah.

MISHNAH, AVOT , OP. CIT., 4:2

Optional Section

Text 13

ולזאת תהיינה נפשו האלהית והחיונית ולבושיהן כולן מיוחדות בתכלית
היחוד ברצון העליון ואור א״ס ב״ה כנ״ל. ויחוד זה למעלה הוא נצחי
לעולם ועד כי הוא ית׳ ורצונו למעלה מהזמן

תניא פרק כה

Thus his soul—both the divine and the animating souls—and their "garments" of thought, speech, and action, will be united in perfect unity with the Divine Will and with the infinite light of G-d, blessed be He.

In the upper spheres, this union [between the soul and G-d] is eternal. For G-d, blessed be He, and His Will transcend time, [and thus the union with G-d and His Will also transcends time and is eternal].

Tanya, op. cit., Chapter 25

Total Redemption

Text 14a

וְעַמֵּךְ כֻּלָּם צַדִּיקִים לְעוֹלָם יִירְשׁוּ אָרֶץ נֵצֶר מַטָּעַי מַעֲשֵׂה יָדַי לְהִתְפָּאֵר

ישעיהו ס,כא

And your people are all righteous; they shall inherit the land forever; they are the branch of My planting, the work of My hands, in which to take pride.

YESHAYAHU/ISAIAH 60:21

Text 14b

Rabbi Naftali Hertz ben Yaakov Elchanan Bachrach (17th century). Born in Frankfurt am Main; German kabbalist; wrote *Emek HaMelech* in order to explain various passages of the *Zohar* and the teachings of the AriZal. The work has had a major impact on later Kabbalah, and is often quoted in Chabad *Chasidut*.

Firstly, they have sparks of holiness in them. They are "My guarded planting," and this G-dly portion that is in them is eternal . . . . The souls are an imprint of G-d's essential light—for He breathed the soul from His innermost self.

Also, they are "the work of My hands in whom to take pride." The work of His hands exists and lives for all eternity. It is impossible for it to cease to exist.

RABBI NAFTALI HERTZ BACHRACH, EMEK HAMELECH, TIKUNEI HATESHUVAH, CHAPTER 3

Key Points

1. Death is the ultimate transition.

2. While transitions can be scary and painful, the process of death and the afterlife are ultimately positive for everyone.

3. Our focus should be on life: preparing now, fulfilling our life mission, and keeping our priorities straight ease the transition.

4. The pleasure of the afterlife is inherently a G-dly one, transcending all worldly experience and comprehension. This is why the soul must undergo a process of disassociation from the body and world before experiencing Paradise.

5. We create our Paradise through our deeds on earth. Each mitzvah unites us eternally with G-d's Essence.

6. Thus, we accomplish a greater union with G-d on earth, but we appreciate and experience the effects of our work more in heaven.

7. Every Jew has share in Paradise, because the soul's essence is G-dly. Life and death only serve to reveal this bond, but can never sever it.

8. Our main focus must be on living life to its fullest—a life full of meaning and mitzvot.

Additional Readings

Life After Death

By **Rabbi Maurice Lamm**

Man ha's had an abiding faith in a world beyond the grave. The conviction in a life after death, improvable but unshakeable, has been cherished since the beginning of thinking man's life on earth. It makes its appearance in religious literature not as fiat, commanded irrevocably by an absolute God, but rather arises plant-like, growing and developing naturally in the soul. It then sprouts forth through sublime prayer and sacred hymn. Only later does it become extrapolated in complicated metaphysical speculation.

The after-life has not been "thought up"; it is not a rational construction of a religious philosophy imposed on believing man. It has sprung from within the hearts of masses of men, a sort of consensus Pentium, inside out, a hope beyond and above the rational, a longing for the warm sun of eternity. The after-life is not a theory to be proven logically or demonstrated by rational analysis. It is axiomatic. It is to the soul what oxygen is to the lungs. There is little meaning to life, to God, to man's constant strivings, to all of his achievements, unless there is a world beyond the grave.

The Bible, so vitally concerned with the actions of man in this world, and agonizing over his day-to-day morals, is relatively silent about the world-to-come. But, precisely, this very silence is a tribute to the awesome concept, taken for granted like the oxygen in the atmosphere. No elaborate apologia, no complex abstractions are necessary. The Bible, which records the sacred dialogue between God and man, surely must be founded on the soul's eternal existence. It was not a matter of debate, as it became later in history when whole movements interpreted scripture with slavish literalism and could not find the after-life crystallized in letters and words, or later, when philosophers began to apply the yardstick of rationalism to man's every hope and idea and sought empirical proof for this conviction of the soul. It was a fundamental creed, always present, though rarely articulated.

If the soul is immortal then death cannot be considered a final act. If the life of the soul is to be continued, then death, however bitter, is deprived of its treacherous power of casting mourners into a lifetime of agonizing hopelessness over an irretrievable loss. Terrible though it is, death is a threshold to a new world—the "world-to-come."

A Parable

An imaginative and telling analogy that conveys the hope and confidence in the after-life, even though this hope must be refracted through the prism of death, is the tale of twins awaiting birth in the mother's womb. It was created by a contemporary Israeli rabbi, the late Y. M. Tuckachinsky.

Imagine twins growing peacefully in the warmth of the womb. Their mouths are closed, and they are being fed via the navel. Their lives are serene. The whole world, to these brothers, is the interior of the womb. Who could conceive anything larger, better, more comfortable? They begin to wonder: "We are getting lower and lower. Surely if it continues, we will exit one day. What will happen after we exit?"

Now the first infant is a believer. He is heir to a religious tradition which tells him that there will be a "new life" after this wet and warm existence of the womb. A strange belief, seemingly without foundation, but one to which he holds fast. The second infant is a thorough-going skeptic. Mere stories do not deceive him. He believes only in that which can be demonstrated. He is enlightened, and tolerates no idle conjecture. What is not within one's experience can have no basis in one's imagination.

Says the faithful brother: "After our 'death' here, there will be a new great world. We will eat through the mouth! We will see great distances, and we will hear through the ears on the sides of our heads. Why, our feet will be straightened! And our heads-up and free, rather than down and boxed in."

Replies the skeptic: "Nonsense. You're straining your imagination again. There is no foundation for this belief. It is only your survival instinct, an elaborate defense mechanism, a historically-conditioned subterfuge. You are looking for something to calm your fear of 'death.' There is only this world. There is no world-to-come!"

"Well then," asks the first, "what do you say it will be like?"

The second brother snappily replies with all the assurance of the slightly knowledgeable: "We will go with a bang. Our world will collapse and we will sink into oblivion. No more. Nothing. Black void. An end to consciousness. Forgotten. This may not be a comforting thought, but it is a logical one."

Suddenly the water inside the womb bursts. The womb convulses. Upheaval. Turmoil. Writhing. Everything lets loose. Then a mysterious pounding—a crushing, staccato pounding. Faster, faster, lower, lower.

The believing brother exits. Tearing himself from the womb, he falls outward. The second brother shrieks, startled by the "accident" befallen his brother. He bewails and bemoans the tragedy—the death of a perfectly fine fellow. Why? Why? Why didn't he take better care? Why did he fall into that terrible abyss?

As he thus laments, he hears a head-splitting cry, and a great tumult from the black abyss, and he trembles: "Oh my! What a horrible end! As I predicted!"

Meanwhile as the skeptic brother mourns, his "dead" brother has been born into the "new" world. The head-splitting cry is a sign of health and vigor, and the tumult is really a chorus of mazel tovs sounded by the waiting family thanking God for the birth of a healthy son.

Indeed, in the words of a contemporary thinker, man comes from the darkness of the "not yet," and proceeds to the darkness of the "no more." While it is difficult to imagine the "not yet" it is more difficult to picture the "no more."

As we separate and "die" from the womb, only to be born to life, so we separate and die from our world, only to be re-born to life eternal. The exit from the womb is the birth of the body. The exit from the body is the birth of the soul. As the womb requires a gestation period of nine months, the world requires a residence of 70 or 80 years. As the womb is prozdor, an anteroom preparatory to life, so our present existence is a prozdor to the world beyond.

This is an excerpt from *The Jewish Way in Death and Mourning,* by Rabbi Maurice Lamm.

Reprinted with permission from www.chabad.org

The Resurrection of the Dead

By **Rabbi Maurice Lamm**

The body returns to the earth, dust to dust, but the soul returns to God who gave it. This doctrine of the immortality of the soul is affirmed not only by Judaism and other religions, but by many secular philosophers as well. Judaism, however, also believes in the eventual resurrection of the body, which will be reunited with the soul at a later time on a "great and awesome day of the Lord." The human form of the righteous men of all ages, buried and long since decomposed, will be resurrected at God's will.

The most dramatic portrayal of this bodily resurrection is to be found in the "Valley of Dry Bones" prophecy in Ezekiel 37, read as the Haftorah on the Intermediate Sabbath of Passover. It recalls past deliverances and envisions the future redemption of Israel and the eventual quickening of the dead:

The hand of the Lord was upon me, and the Lord carried me out in a spirit, and set me down in the midst of the valley, and it was full of bones; and He caused me to pass by them round about, and, behold, there were very many in the open valley; and, lo, they were very dry.

And He said unto me: "Son of man, can these bones live?" And I answered: "O Lord, God, Thou knowest."

Then He said unto me: "Prophesy over these bones, and say unto them: 'O ye dry bones, hear the word of the Lord: Thus saith the Lord God unto these bones: Behold, I will cause breath to enter into you, and ye shall live. And I will lay sinews upon you, and will bring up flesh upon you, and cover you with skin, and put breath in you, and ye shall live; and ye shall know that I am the Lord.'"

So I prophesied as I was commanded; and as I prophesied, there was a noise, and behold a commotion, and the bones came together, bone to its bone.

And I beheld, and, lo, there were sinews upon them and flesh came up, and skin covered them above; but there was no breath in them.

Then said He unto me: "Prophesy unto the breath, prophesy, son of man, and say to the breath: 'Thus saith the Lord God: Come from the four winds, O breath, and breathe upon these slain, that they may live.'"

So I prophesied as He commanded me, and the breath came into them, and they lived, and stood upon their feet, an exceeding great host.

Then He said unto me: "Son of man, these bones are the whole house of Israel; behold, they say: 'Our bones are dried up, and our hope is lost; we can clean cut off.'

Therefore, prophesy, and say unto them: 'Thus saith the Lord God: Behold, I will open your graves, and cause you to come up out of your graves, O my people; and I will bring you into the land of Israel. And ye shall know that I am the Lord, when I have opened your graves, and caused you to come up out of your graves, O My people. And I will put My spirit in you, and ye shall live, and I will place you in your own land; and ye shall know that I the Lord have spoken, and performed it, saith the Lord.'"

The power of this conviction can be gauged not only by the quality of the lives of the Jews, their tenacity and gallantry in the face of death, but in the very real fear instilled in their enemies. After destroying Jerusalem and callously decimating its Jewish population, Titus, the Roman general, returned home with only a portion of his Tenth Legion. When asked whether he had lost all of his other men on the battlefield, Titus gave assurance that his men were alive, but that they were still on combat duty. He had left them to stand guard over Jewish corpses in the fields of Jerusalem because he was sincerely afraid that their bodies would be resurrected and they would reconquer the Holy Land as they had promised.

The belief in a bodily resurrection appears, at first sight, to be incredible to the contemporary mind. But when approached from the God's-eye view, why is rebirth more miraculous than birth? The adhesion of sperm and egg, the subsequent fertilization and development in the womb culminating in the birth of the astoundingly complex network of tubes and glands, bones and organs, their incredibly precise functioning and the unbelievably intricate human brain that guides them, is surely a miracle of the first magnitude. Curiously, the miraculous object, man himself, takes this for granted. In his preoccupation with daily trivia, he ignores the miracle of his own existence. The idea of rebirth may appear strange because we have never experienced a similar occurrence, for which reason we cannot put together the stuff of imagination. Perhaps it is because we can be active in creating life, but cannot participate with God in the recreation of life. Perhaps it is because, scientifically, recreation flies against any biological theory, while we are slowly coming to know how life is developed, and our researchers are about to create life in the laboratory test tube. But, who has created the researching biologist? And, can we not postulate an omnipotent Divine Biologist who created all men? Surely resurrection is not beyond the capacity of an omnipotent God.

The sages simplified the concept of bodily resurrection by posing an analogy which brings it within the experience of man. A tree, once alive with blossoms and fruit, full of the sap of life, stands cold and still in the winter. Its leaves have browned and fallen, its fruit rots on the ground. But the warm rains come and the sun shines. Buds sprout. Green leaves appear. Colorful fruits burst from their seed. With the coming of spring, God resurrects nature. For this reason the blessing of God for reviving the dead, which is recited in every daily Amidah, incorporates also the seasonal requests for rain. When praying for the redemption of man, the prayerbook uses the phrase *matzmi'ach yeshuah*, "planting salvation." Indeed, the Talmud compares the day of resurrection with the rainy season, and notes that the latter is even more significant—for resurrection serves only the righteous while the rain falls indiscriminately on all men.

This is one supplementary reason why the body and all its limbs require to be interred in the earth and not cremated, for it expresses our faith in the future resurrection. Naturally, the all-powerful God can recreate the body whether it was buried or drowned or burned. Yet, willful cremation signifies an arrogant denial of the possibility of resurrection, and those who deny this cardinal principle should not share in the reward for its observance. The body and its limbs—whether amputated before death, or during a permissible post-mortem examination—have to be allowed to decompose as one complete organism by the processes of nature, not by man's mechanical act.

Resurrection: A Symbolic Idea

Some contemporary thinkers have noted that the physical revival of the dead is symbolic of a cluster of basic Jewish ideas:

First, man does not achieve the ultimate redemption by virtue of his own inherent nature. It is not because he, uniquely, possesses an immortal soul that he, inevitably, will be resurrected. The concept of resurrection underscores man's reliance on God who, in the words of the prayerbook, "Wakes the dead in great mercy." It is His grace and His mercy that rewards the deserving, and revives those who sleep in the dust.

Second, resurrection is not only a private matter, a bonus for the righteous individual. It is a corporate reward. All of the righteous of all ages, those who stood at Sinai, and those of our generation, will be revived. The community of the righteous has a corporate and historic character. It will live again as a whole people. The individual, even in death, is not separated from the society in which he lived.

Third, physical resurrection affirms unequivocally that man's soul and his body are the creations of a holy God. There is a tendency to assume that the affirmation of a spiritual dimension in man must bring with it the

corollary that his physical being is depreciated. Indeed, such has been the development of the body-soul duality in both the Christian tradition and in Oriental religions, and accounts for their glorification of asceticism. Further, even the Greek philosophers, who were enamored of the beauty of the body, came to denigrate the physical side of man. They crowned reason as man's noblest virtue. For them the spiritual intellectual endeavor to perceive the unchanging truth was the highest function of man. Man's material existence, on the other hand, was always in flux, subject to change and, therefore, inferior. Thus, they accepted immortality of the soul—which to the Greeks was what we call mind—which survives the extinction of his physical being. But they could not understand physical resurrection because they did not, by any means, consider the body worthy of being reborn.

To the contrary, Judaism has always stressed that the body, as the soul, is a gift of God—indeed, that it belongs to God. *Ha'neshamah lach ve'haguf pa'alach*, the Jew declared, "The soul is yours, and the body is your handiwork." To care for the body is a religious command of the Bible. The practice of asceticism for religious purposes was tolerated, but the ascetic had to bring a sacrifice of atonement for his action. Resurrection affirms that the body is of value because it came from God, and it will be revived by God. Resurrection affirms that man's empirical existence is valuable in God's eyes. His activities in this world are significant in the scheme of eternity. His strivings are not to be deprecated as vain and useless, but are to be brought to fulfillment at the end of days.

The concept of resurrection thus serves to keep God ever in man's consciousness, to unify contemporary and historic Jewry, to affirm the value of God's world, and to heighten, rather than to depress, the value of man's worthy strivings in this world.

Which specific virtues might guarantee a person's resurrection is a subject of much debate. The method of resurrection is, of course, an open question that invites conjecture, but which can offer no definite answer.

While the details of the after-life are thus very much a matter of speculation, the traditional consensus must serve to illuminate the dark path. In the words of Rabbi Joshua ben Chanania (Niddah 10b): "When they come to life again, we will consult about the matter."

This is an excerpt from *The Jewish Way in Death and Mourning*, by Rabbi Maurice Lamm.
Reprinted with permission from www.chabad.org

In Sorrow and in Joy

By **Mrs. Esther Wachsman**

I am quite aware of the fact that I am here, an ordinary woman, wife, mother and teacher from Israel, for the sole reason that I am Nachshon's mother. I realize that our personal tragedy has become the tragedy of the Jewish people. Our son Nachshon has become everybody's child, and I have become a symbol of the mothers of Israel—a mother who has been called upon to make the greatest sacrifice and to cope with a tragedy that no mother should ever have to cope with.

The subject of this talk is "Reaching Beyond Limitations." What are limitations? We are all limited. The famous chasidic story of Reb Zushya of Anipoli teaches us that the heavenly court will not ask, "Why weren't you as great as Abraham, Isaac, or Jacob?" but rather, "Why weren't you Zushya—why weren't you the best Zushya you could possibly be?"

Several months ago I was given an honorary doctorate by Yeshiva University, and one of my fellow honorees was Professor Branover, the renowned scientist from Israel. He was told by the Rebbe before addressing a conference of Jewish scientists to convey to following message: As a scholar of solar energy, you must encourage every Jew to emulate the sun. Though there are larger heavenly bodies which dwarf the sun in size, the sun is unique for it provides light and generates heat. Celestial phenomena, such as black holes are powerful sources of energy, but that energy is directed inward. The black holes pull the energy they emit to themselves. The sun, by contrast, gives of itself to the entire planetary system. So too, must a Jew radiate *Ahavat Yisrael*. If the sun was only heating its own mass, who would have paid it any attention?

[In our own lives,] we reached out from our black hole of despair to our fellow Jews and tried to radiate love for them and closeness with our brothers. We called on our people to pray, to light a Shabbat candle, to unite with us. So though my family and I are not officially Lubavitcher Chasidim, I am proud to consider myself a qualified Chasid of your great Rebbe's message, which in our own humble way we tried to fulfill.

Now, what was my personal limit? Was it when I learned that my husband was experiencing kidney failure and would have to undergo dialysis? At that time, we had a one year old baby and four other children aged five through ten. Was it four years later, when, at the height of my husband's illness, while we were desperately waiting for a kidney donor, I gave birth to twin boys and was informed that one of the babies had Down's syndrome? Was it when our son was kidnapped and murdered by Hamas terrorists? Certainly I felt devastated, grief stricken, and severely depressed by all of these events.

And yes, I questioned G-d. I did not understand. I could not understand, and I have given much thought and study to the eternal questions of the suffering of the innocent, of unanswered prayers. And I would like to share some of my thoughts with you.

It all starts with the assumption that most of us have that we are entitled to have good things happen to us. We, who are good, observant Jews who fulfill our part of the bargain, then expect G-d to fulfill his part, and grant our wishes as a reward for our piety.

This assumption is based on the prior assumption that everything that happens to us is a reward or punishment for things we did. But I have learned that a basic message of Judaism is that there is no guarantee at any point, that the wishes of G-d and those of man will coincide. As it is written in Kohelet [Ecclesiastes]: ". . . In thy days of good fortune be joyful, and in thy days of adversity consider; G-d has made the one as well as the other, and man cannot know what lies in store for him."

We are in this world to confront challenges; to choose, when we are tested, to remain firm in our belief and trust in G-d, in every situation. As a great philosopher once said: "He who has a why to live for, can bear any how."

As philosopher, author and holocaust survivor Viktor Frankl stated in his famous book *Man's Search For Meaning*: "There is nothing in the world that would effectively help one to survive the worst conditions as the knowledge that there is meaning in one's life."

In a G-d-created world, nothing is random or meaningless. The world is not a conglomeration of coincidence and chance. There is a meaning and a purpose in existence and each one of us is here, for a purpose, to do a task in this world.

I would like to talk to you about the possible meaning of Nachshon's life and death.

Nachshon was the third of our seven sons and the third to serve in the Golani brigade of the IDF: He had to outdo his older brothers and therefore joined an elite commando branch of Golani after his yeshiva studies. He was the smallest and thinnest of those boys in his unit and they used to call him their baby. He was the one who always boosted their spirits with his ready smile and eternal optimism. He spent four months in Lebanon and he kept them going, as they all told us later, when their sergeant was killed. When Nachshon's friend from the neighborhood was killed within inches of him, he came home and said Hagomel, he had been spared.

Let me tell you what it is like to be the mother of a son in Lebanon, a boy of nineteen, for he was only a boy. It means eating, drinking, breathing "Lebanon" every waking moment and sleeping with a radio attached to your ear, waiting to hear what happened, who was killed, who was wounded. When the names of the dead and wounded are released, you cry with their families, yet you are relieved that it wasn't your child this time.

Nachshon didn't lose his life in battle. No, Nachshon was brutally murdered exactly 50 years after all his ancestors, my grandparents, aunts, uncles, cousins, met their deaths in the ovens of Nazi Germany for the same reason—because he was a Jew. This time a proud Jew in his own country, wearing his country's uniform, kidnapped in the heart of Israel just a few miles from Ben Gurion Airport.

Nachshon's naive, trusting, happy nature did not allow him to suspect the fatal car that stopped to give him a ride home. A car with four men wearing yarmulkes with chasidic music playing on the tape deck, and a Tanakh and siddur on the dashboard.

When Nachshon did not come home on Sunday night from a one day army course to get a license to operate a special vehicle for his unit, we were very concerned. If our sons are delayed for any reason, they always call their mother. And so when by late Sunday night Nachshon had not called or returned, we feared the worst and already, at that time, notified the authorities. On Monday, there were search parties looking for him in the area where he had last been seen. By Monday, for me my son was dead. And so paradoxically, when on Tuesday afternoon we were notified by Israel television of the video tape showing his capture by Hamas terrorists, contrary to the national feelings of horror and despair, I felt relief and joy and optimism. He was alive. There was no place for grief and sorrow at this point. We were mobilized around the clock to do everything in our power to save Nachshon. We contacted Muslim religious leaders who appealed to his captors and forbade them to harm him. We announced his American citizenship and the U.S. government intervened. We begged our Prime Minister to negotiate and he—and we too—spoke to chairman Arafat who promised to do everything he could to find our son. We spoke constantly to the media all over the world and many heads of state. We contacted Arab leaders who all told his captors to release Nachshon unharmed. We spoke to the media believing and hoping that Nachshon could hear us. And we remained hopeful, knowing we were doing everything in our power for him.

The unity and solidarity among our people at that time is almost unprecedented in recent memory. All of the Jewish left-wingers, religious and secular, young and old, rich and poor, Sephardi and Ashkenazai prayed with us. Every school child in Israel said three chapters of Tehillim. . . . Chasidim swayed and cried side by side with boys in torn jeans, pony tails and earrings. And at that same time, Jewish people around the world held prayer vigils for his safety.

My home was filled with members of the Knesset, ministers, mayors and soldiers, along with teachers, students, truck drivers and laborers. We were one people, one Jewish soul praying for one Jewish child who had become everyone's child, brother and friend. . . . indeed, Israeli radio began each morning's broadcast with the words: "Good morning Israel. We are all the Wachsman Family."

On Friday, hours before the terrorists' ultimatum, before lighting the Sabbath candles, I appealed to all Jewish women in the world to light a candle for my son before Shabbat. I have received thousands of letters from women who had never lit candles before, saying that they had done so for my son. The outpouring of love from around the world brought me much comfort. . .

I sat at the Shabbat table that Friday night with my eyes glued to the door, certain that Nachshon would walk in at any moment. For surely all those prayers of the whole Jewish people would shake the heavens. But as you all know, that was not to be.

Instead, General Yoram Yair walked through the door, and we knew what message he was bringing us. We had not known of the government's decision to implement its military option and storm the hideout where Nachshon was being held captive, a house just a few miles away from his own home, which our intelligence had discovered only hours earlier. Unknown to us at the time, our quiet neighborhood streets were thronged with hundreds of people, many of whom were our friends and neighbors who waited to hear some word of Nachshon's fate. Because it was the Sabbath, they could not put on the television or radio, and many heard the news when we did, over the radios of army vehicles protecting security. At that same time, our own sons, and hundreds of our neighbors were still in our synagogue saying Tehillim when the terrible news was brought to us.

Many of those same people, children and adults, then questioned why G-d had not answered all their fervent prayers. . . . At the eulogy at Nachshon's funeral, his Rosh Yeshiva said that G-d did hear our prayers, and did answer, but that His answer this time was "No." Just as a parent must sometimes say no to his child, no matter how much he begs for a positive answer, and the child cannot understand why his parent says no, so we, G-d's

children, could not understand why G-d said no, but we accept his will and remember and are grateful for all the times he said "Yes," and gave me health, a beautiful family, the privilege to live in Jerusalem, and many moments of joy. No mere mortal can understand G-d's way and his running of the universe. Moses asked to see His face and was told "no one can see my face and live." That is, no mere mortal can understand my ways and how I run the universe. Job suffered greatly: he lost his children, his wealth, and finally his health. His so-called friends and comforters told him that he must have sinned to bring down such a fate upon himself, but G-d tells him this is not so. He has not been punished for any sins. But G-d, who created the universe in all its magnificence, decides what shall happen and how to run the world.

In all of our history, sorrow and joy, grief and rejoicing, mourning and comfort, life and death, destruction and rebuilding are intertwined. We know that darkness and light are mixed together and sometimes we do not know which is which. Man's purpose is to endure, to cope, to rebuild, to believe in G-d's master plan for the universe and to trust that every aspect of life has meaning and takes the course G-d had determined.

After the destruction of the temple, G-d asks the prophet Jeremiah to comfort Him, but the prophet can find no words, for no one can comfort a bereaved parent. But G-d himself finds the words of comfort, and says, "It will yet be heard in the cities of Judah and the outskirts of Jerusalem. . . ."

Just a few months after the darkest period our family has ever known, we danced at two of our sons' weddings, and the *Bar-Mitzvah* of a third. All those who sat with us during shiva, returned to dance with us in our joy. As we accepted G-d's will in our tragedy, so we accepted His will in bringing us joy, and did not allow one to cancel out the other. We lived the expression: One must bless the Almighty in sorrow as we bless Him in our joy.

. . . The Yizkor and Kaddish prayer for the dead is a reaffirmation of G-d's glory. When our faith is stretched to the limit, when we are asked to overcome the greatest of limitations, that is when we must remember to praise G-d.

May I conclude with the words of the prophet Zechariah: "Death shall be vanquished forever, and G-d shall wipe the tears from all faces."

And so we await the final redemption, the coming of *Moshiach*, *Techiyat Hamaytim*, when we will be reunited with our loved ones.

From the keynote address by Mrs. Esther Wachsman at the International Lubavitch Women's Convention in Toronto, Canada, January 1996.

Reprinted by www.chabad.org with permission from *Wellsprings* magazine, a publication of Lubavitch Youth Organization.

Reprinted here with permission from www.chabad.org

Lesson 4
Have You Been Here Before?

Introduction

Was I someone else in a different life? Do souls return to this world in another body to complete unfinished business? Can a previous life affect my present and my future?

In Lesson Four of *Soul Quest,* we explore Kabbalah's unique understanding of reincarnation. We will discover a complex system of interconnectedness between souls, and the ways that one soul influences and even spawns another.

Learning Activity 1

True or False?

Circle the best answers to these questions about reincarnation.

1. Belief in reincarnation is a basic part of Judaism. T F

2. (Jewish) reincarnation means that the same soul that once inhabited one body returns to inhabit another body. T F

3. Reincarnated souls do not have their own identity, but share their identity with someone who lived in a previous lifetime. T F

4. The purpose of doing good in one's current lifetime is in order to be reincarnated as a person of higher status in a future reincarnation. T F

5. Souls are reincarnated in order to punish the soul for sins done in a past life. T F

Have You Been Here Before?

Text 1

Know that even though you will frequently find references in many places stating "this person was reincarnated into that one and subsequently, into someone else," do not err by thinking that the original soul is the one that is reincarnated. Rather, a number of "root souls" without limit were divided into souls, and in each of these "root souls"

Rabbi Yitschak Luria (1534–1572). Known by the acronym AriZal or simply the Ari. Founder of the Lurianic school of Kabbalah. Born in Jerusalem; raised in Egypt; died in Safed. Rabbi Luria studied Talmud under Rabbi Betzalel Ashkenazi, compiler of the *Shitah Mekubetzet*. Despite his youth, he was accepted among the rabbinic elite of Safed. The *Ari* never recorded his teachings; they were collected and transcribed by his disciples. His leading disciple, Rabbi Chaim Vital, is generally considered the most authoritative recorder of the AriZal's teachings. His primary work is his *Eitz Chaim*.

there are a number of sparks of souls without limit, and in each incarnation, some of these sparks are rectified. And those that are not rectified return to be reincarnated and to become rectified. But those sparks that have already been rectified rise up to the [spiritual] level that befits them.

RABBI YITSCHAK LURIA, SHAAR HAGILGULIM, HAKDAMAH 14

From One to Many and Back to One

Text 2a

First there was one soul, father to all of them, and this was the soul of Adam. Afterwards, all souls were included in the souls of the three patriarchs, Avraham/Abraham, Yitschak/Isaac, and Yaakov/Jacob. After that, they were all divided into the souls of the seventy [members of Yaakov's family who descended to Egypt]. Then, the seventy souls were divided into six-hundred thousand great sparks.

SHAAR HAGILGULIM, OP. CIT., HAKDAMAH 11

Text 2b 🔳

כל הנשמה ונפש האלהית שבכל ישראל המתחלקת בפרטות לששים רבוא
. . . אלא ששים רבוא נשמות פרטיות אלו הן שרשי׳ וכל שרש מתחלק
לששים רבוא ניצוצות שכל ניצוץ הוא נשמה אחת

תניא פרק לז

The whole *neshamah*, the Divine soul in all of Israel, is divided into 600,000 particular offshoots. . . . These 600,000 particular souls, however, are roots, and each root-soul differentiates into 600,000 sparks, each spark being one *neshamah*.

RABBI SHNE'UR ZALMAN OF LIADI, TANYA, CHAPTER 37

Rabbi Shne'ur Zalman of Liadi (1745–1812). Known as "the Alter Rebbe" and "the Rav"; Born in Liozna, Belarus; buried in Hadiach, Ukraine; chassidic Rebbe and founder of the Chabad movement; among the principal students of the Magid of Mezeritch. His numerous works include the *Tanya*, an early classic of Chassidism; *Torah Or* and *Likutei Torah*; and *Shulchan Aruch HaRav*, a rewritten code of Jewish law. He was succeeded by his son, Rabbi Dovber of Lubavitch.

Text 2c 🔳

The six vectors (representing the six *sefirot* of *Ze'ir Anpin*) each contain ten . . . .

The source of the 600,000 is thus derived from the four-letter name of G-d. Six is the *vav*, times ten, which is the *yud*, to the fifth power, which is the *hey*.

$$6 \times (10^5) = 600,000$$

RABBI SHNE'UR ZALMAN OF LIADI,
SEFER HAMA'AMARIM 5566, VOL. 2, P. 438 FF.

Text 3 ❚

The connection of the soul to G-d is compared to a cord comprising 613 strands. The soul is compared to a cord, for it is the soul that connects man to G-d. The 613 strands are the 613 faculties of the soul . . . .

[Why does the soul have 613 components?]

Man is structured with 248 parts and 365 veins, a total of 613 components. The universe is a macrocosm of the person, which is why throughout all of the spiritual realms, everything is comprised of this number.

This is also true of the soul, which explains why the soul has 613 faculties, to which the 613 commandments correspond.

This soul is the cord connecting a person to G-d. Just like a cord connects two opposite ends making them one, similarly, the soul has one end connected above . . . and the other end attached below. This refers to the "reflection" of the soul, which is enclothed in the body and gives it life.

RABBI YOSEF YITSCHAK SCHNEERSOHN, BATI LEGANI, 5710, CHAPTER 4

Rabbi Yosef Yitschak Schneersohn (1880–1950). Also known by the acronym *Rayyatz*, or as the "Previous (or Frierdike) Rebbe"; Son of Rabbi Sholom Dovber Schneersohn; chassidic Rebbe and sixth leader of the Chabad–Lubavitch movement. Rabbi Schneersohn's activities in defense of Russian Jewry led to his arrest by both Czarist and Communist authorities. After liberation from Soviet prison and exile, he moved to Riga, Latvia and later Warsaw, Poland. From there he fled during the Nazi occupation of Poland and eventually arrived in New York in 1940. Settling in Crown Heights, Brooklyn, Rabbi Schneersohn worked to revitalize American Jewish life. His son-in-law, Rabbi Menachem Mendel Schneerson, succeeded him as leader of the Chabad movement.

Text 4 📖

כאשר כל הנשמה ונפש האלהית שבכל ישראל המתחלקת בפרטות לששים
רבוא תקיים כל נפש פרטית כל תרי"ג מצות התורה שס"ה ל"ת . . . שלא
יינקו ויקבלו חיות בעבירה זו . . . ורמ"ח מצות עשה להמשיך אור א"ס ב"ה
למטה להעלות לו ולקשר וליחד בו כללות הנפש החיונית שברמ"ח אברי
הגוף ביחוד גמור להיות לאחדים ממש כמו שעלה ברצונו ית' להיות לו
דירה בתחתונים . . . ומאחר שכללות נפש החיונית שבכללות ישראל תהיה
מרכבה קדושה לה' אזי גם כללות החיות של עו"הז תצא אז מטומאתה
וחלאתה ותעלה לקדושה להיות מרכבה לה' בהתגלות כבודו וראו כל בשר
יחדיו (ישעי' מ,ה) ויופיע עליהם בהדר גאון עוזו וימלא כבוד ה' את כל הארץ
תניא פרק לז

The Divine soul in all of Israel . . . is divided into
600,000 particular offshoots.

[When] each individual soul therein will fulfill
all the 613 mitzvot of the Torah . . . [by refraining from
transgressing] the 365 prohibitions . . . so that they do
not draw nurture or receive vitality by means of such
transgression . . . .

[And by observing] the 248 positive commandments,
thereby drawing down the blessed *Ein Sof* below, to
unite with Him the entire vital soul, which is in the 248
limbs of the body, in perfect unity, so that they become
actually one [with Him], in accordance with His Will
that there be an abode for Him in the lower realms . . . .

Once the totality of the vital soul of the community of
Israel will become a holy vehicle for G-d, then also the
general vitality of this world . . . will also emerge from

its impurity and [will] ascend to holiness, to become a vehicle for G-d, upon the revelation of His glory [in the world to come].

"And [then] all flesh will behold [G-dliness] together [Yeshayahu/Isaiah 40:5]," and He will shine forth upon them with the majestic beauty of His power, and the glory of G-d will fill the whole world.

TANYA, CHAPTER 37, OP. CIT.

Text 5

Know, too, that a person must observe all 613 commandments, in thought, speech, and action . . . and if the person does not fulfill all 613 in each of the three dimensions mentioned, then the person will need to be reincarnated until they are completed.

SHAAR HAGILGULIM, OP. CIT., HAKDAMAH 15

Text 6

The Sages of the true [wisdom] also taught that in order to perfect itself, every soul must engage in all the parts [of the Torah] according to its capacity to comprehend and perceive. Any person with the potential to comprehend and perceive much, but due to indolence comprehended and perceived only little, must reincarnate until he comprehends and perceives everything that his soul can comprehend and perceive in the knowledge of the Torah. This includes the *Peshat* [simple meaning of] the laws, the *Remez* [hinted meaning], the *Drush* [interpretive, analytical meaning], and the *Sod* [mystical meaning]. For whatever the soul can comprehend and perceive in the knowledge of the Torah consummates its perfection. It cannot reach consummate perfection in the Bond of Life—G-d in the Source from which it was hewn—without this knowledge. Therefore our Sages declared: "Happy is he who arrives here [to Gan Eden in the spiritual realms] with his knowledge in hand," so that he will not have to reincarnate and [descend] again to this [material] world.

Rabbi Shne'ur Zalman of Liadi,
Code of Jewish Law, laws of Torah Study 1:4

Text 7

As we have already said, a person is obligated to learn Torah on all four levels. Now, there are only 600,000 souls, and the Torah itself is the source of all Jewish souls, the place from which they are "hewn." Therefore, there are 600,000 explanations on the level of *Peshat*, on the level of *Remez*, on the level of *Drush*, and on the level of *Sod*.

Thus, for every one of the 600,000 explanations there is one Jewish soul, and in the time to come each will know Torah according to the explanation that corresponds to the root of his soul. In *Gan Eden*, after a person has died, he will understand all of it.

SHAAR HAGILGULIM, OP. CIT., HAKDAMAH 17

Rabbi Menachem Azariah of Fano (1548–1620). Also known as Immanuel da Fano. Born in Fano, Italy; passed away in Mantua; among the disciples of Rabbi Moshe Cordovero; rabbi, talmudist, and kabbalist of note. A patron of learning, Rabbi da Fano helped bring Rabbi Yosef Caro's *Kesef Mishneh*, his commentary on Maimonides' *Mishneh Torah*, to print. Rabbi Chaim Yosef David Azulai enumerates, in *Shem HaGedolim*, twenty-four kabbalistic treatises by Rabbi da Fano, ten of which are included in da Fano's noted work, *Asarah Ma'amarot.*

Text 8

Devorah/Deborah the prophetess was a re-incarnation of Tsiporah, the wife of our teacher Moshe/Moses (may he rest in peace), because at the time that the Jewish people sang praises [to G-d] at the sea, she was not with them, and she was pained by this.

RABBI MENACHEM AZARIAH OF FANO, GILGULEI NESHAMOT, LIKUTIM 3

How Do We Know?

Text 9

Ever since G-d told our father Avraham, "Go from your land, [etc.] (Bereishit/Genesis 12:1)," and it is then written, "Avram kept travelling southward (Bereishit 12:9)," we have the beginning of the mystery of rectifying the sparks. By decree of Divine Providence, people travel to the place where the sparks that they must purify await their redemption.

RABBI MENACHEM MENDEL SCHNEERSON, HAYOM YOM, CHESHVAN I

Rabbi Menachem Mendel Schneerson (1902–1994). Known as "the Lubavitcher Rebbe," or simply as "the Rebbe." Born in southern Ukraine. Rabbi Schneerson escaped from the Nazis, arriving in the US in June 1941. The towering Jewish leader of the twentieth century, the Rebbe inspired and guided the revival of traditional Judaism after the European devastation, and often emphasized that the performance of just one additional good deed could usher in the era of Mashiach.

Text 10

You tell me you are giving the proper amount of *tzedakah*. However, your *shalom bayit* [harmony in family relationships] situation needs great improvement.

The fact that you are having great difficulties in this area is a sign that this mitzvah has not been completed in your previous life.

The Holy AriZal teaches us that most souls living in a body have been here before. The reason they come back again is to fulfill those mitzvot that they did not do properly the first time around.

Those mitzvot that they did complete in their previous lifetime do not require any more refinement, and therefore their observance is easy. However, those mitzvos that one did not complete in a previous lifetime are the ones most difficult to do. The negative inclination targets these non-completed mitzvot as the ones to oppose most.

The fact that the issue of *shalom bayit* is so difficult for you proves that it is a mitzvah which needs fulfillment. In your past lifetime, you did not refine this mitzvah. Now is your opportunity.

RABBI MENACHEM MENDEL SCHNEERSON, IGEROT KODESH, VOL. 5, #1257

Key Points

1. Reincarnation is not recycling an old soul, but the process of a new offshoot continuing the mission begun by a general soul.

2. Jews are united in three ways: (a) they stem from a single source; (b) they function as many organs of a single organism working together for a common goal; and (c) they will ultimately reveal the essence that unites them all, by revealing G-d's oneness in creation.

3. We all share a common source and goal, but we each have our own unique identity and personal assignment, within the global mission.

4. Each root soul must fulfill every mitzvah and learn all of Torah in order to completely reveal the G-dliness in that soul and in its portion of the world.

5. When every root soul completes this process, this brings Mashiach.

6. We are given our specific talents and possessions, and we are each guided through life based on our own unique missions.

7. Areas in life that come easily to us are those that were already rectified in a previous *gilgul*. Those areas that are difficult still need to be refined.

8. Understanding *gilgulim* helps us see the fusion of a global plan with our personal life.

Additional Readings

What Happens After We Die?

By **Rabbi Shlomo Yaffe** and **Rabbi Yanki Tauber**

One of the fundamental beliefs of Judaism is that life does not begin with birth nor end with death. This is articulated in the verse in Kohelet (Ecclesiastes), "And the dust returns to the earth as it was, and the spirit returns to G-d, who gave it."[1]

The Lubavitcher Rebbe would often point out that a basic law of physics (known as the First Law of Thermodynamics) is that no energy is ever "lost" or destroyed; it only assumes another form. If such is the case with physical energy, how much more so a spiritual entity such as the soul, whose existence is not limited by time and space nor any of the other delineators of the physical state. Certainly, the spiritual energy that in the human being is the source of sight and hearing, emotion and intellect, will and consciousness does not cease to exist merely because the physical body has ceased to function; rather, it passes from one form of existence (physical life as expressed and acted via the body) to higher, exclusively spiritual form of existence.

While there are numerous stations in a soul's journey, these can generally be grouped into four general phases:

i) the wholly spiritual existence of the soul before it enters the body;

ii) physical life;

iii) post-physical life in *Gan Eden* (the "Garden of Eden," also called "Heaven" and "Paradise");

iv) the "World to Come" (*Olam HaBa*) that follows the resurrection of the dead.

What are these four phases and why are all four necessary?

To See or Not to See: The Free Choice Paradox

As discussed at length in Chassidic teaching,[2] the ultimate purpose of the soul is fulfilled during the time it spends in this physical world making this world "a dwelling place for G-d" by finding and expressing G-dliness in everyday life through its fulfillment of the mitzvot.

But for our actions in this world to have true significance, they must be the product of our free choice. If we were to experience the power and beauty of the Divine presence we bring into the world with our mitzvot, we would always choose what is right and thereby lose our autonomy. *The obvious becomes robotic.* Our accomplishments would not be ours, any more than it is an "accomplishment" that we eat three meals a day and avoid jumping into fire.

Hence, this crucial stage of our lives is enacted under the conditions of almost total spiritual blackout: in a world in which the Divine reality is hidden, in which our purpose in life is not obvious; a world in which "all its affairs are severe and evil and wicked men prevail."[3] In such a world, our positive and G-dly actions would be truly our own choice and achievement.

On the other hand, however, how would it be possible to discover, and act upon, goodness and truth under such conditions at all? If the soul is plunged into such a G-dless world and cut off from all knowledge of the Divine, by what means could it ever discover the path of truth?

This is why the soul exists in a purely spiritual state *before* it descends in to this world. In its pre-physical existence, the soul is fortified with the Divine wisdom, knowledge and vision that will empower it in its struggles to transcend and transform the physical reality.

In the words of the Talmud: "The fetus in its mother's womb is taught the entire Torah... When its time comes to emerge into the atmosphere of the world, an angel comes and slaps it on its mouth, making it forget everything."[4]

An obvious question: If we're made to forget it all, why teach it to us in the first place? But herein lies the entire paradox of knowledge and choice: we can't see the truth, we can't even manifestly know it, but at the same time we *do* know it, deep inside us. Deep enough that we can choose to ignore it, but also deep enough that wherever we are and whatever we become we can always choose to unearth it. This, in the final analysis, is choice: our choice to pursue the knowledge implanted in our soul or to suppress it.

The Mutual Exclusivity of Achievement and Reward

Thus the stage is set for Phase II: the tests, trials and tribulations of physical life. The characteristics of the physical—its finiteness, its opaqueness, its self-centeredness, its tendency to conceal what lies behind it—form a heavy veil that obscures virtually all knowledge and memory of our Divine source. And yet, deep down we know right from wrong. Somehow, we know that life is meaningful, that we are here to fulfill a Divine purpose; somehow, when confronted with a choice between a G-dly action and an unG-dly one, we know the difference. The knowledge is faint—a dim, subconscious memory from a prior, spiritual state. We can silence it or amplify it—the choice is ours.

Everything physical is, by definition, finite; indeed, that is what makes it a concealment of the infinitude of the Divine. Intrinsic to physical life is that it is finite in time: it ends. Once it ends—once our soul is freed from its physical embodiment—we can no longer achieve and accomplish. But now, finally, we can behold and derive satisfaction from what we have accomplished.

The two are mutually exclusive: achievement precludes satisfaction; satisfaction precludes achievement. Achievement can only take place in the spiritual blindness of the physical world; satisfaction can only take place in the choice-less environment of the spiritual reality.

The Talmud quotes the verse: "You shall keep the mitzvah, the decrees and the laws which I command you today to do them."[5] "Today to do them," explains the Talmud, "but not to do them tomorrow. Today to do them, and tomorrow to receive their reward."[6] The *Ethics* expresses it thus: "A single moment of repentance and good deeds in this world is greater than all of the world to come. And a single moment of bliss in the world to come is greater than all of this world."[7]

It's as if we spent a hundred years watching an orchestra performing a symphony on television—with the sound turned off. We watched the hand-movements of the conductor and the musicians. Sometimes we asked: why are the people on the screen making all these strange motions to no purpose? Sometimes we understood that a great piece of music was being played, but didn't hear a single note. After a hundred years of watching in silence, we watch it again—this time with the sound turned on.

The orchestra is ourselves, and the music—played well or poorly—are the deeds of our lives.

What Are Heaven and Hell?

Heaven and hell are where the soul receives its punishment and reward after death. Yes, Judaism believes in, and Jewish traditional sources extensively discuss, punishment and reward in the afterlife (indeed, it is one of the "Thirteen Principles" of Judaism enumerated by Maimonides). But these are a very different "heaven" and "hell" than what one finds described in medieval Christian texts or *New Yorker* cartoons. Heaven is not a place of halos and harps, nor is hell populated by those red creatures with pitchforks depicted on the label of non-kosher canned meat.

After death, the soul returns to its Divine Source, together with all the G-dliness it has "extracted" from the physical world by using it for meaningful purposes. The soul now relives its experiences on another plane, and experiences the good it accomplished during its physical lifetime as incredible happiness and pleasure, and the negative as incredibly painful.

This pleasure and pain are not reward and punishment in the conventional sense—in the sense that we might punish a criminal by sending him to jail or reward a dedicated employee with a raise. It is rather that we experience our own life in its reality—a reality from which we were sheltered during our physical lifetimes. We experience the true import and effect of our actions. Turning up the volume on that TV set with that symphony orchestra can be intensely pleasurable or intensely painful,8 depending on how we played the music of our lives.

When the soul departs from the body, it stands before the Heavenly Court to give a "judgment and accounting" of its earthly life.[9] But the Heavenly Court only does the "accounting" part; the "judgment" part—that only the soul itself can do.[10] Only the soul can pass judgment on itself—only it can know and sense the true extent of what it accomplished, or neglected to accomplish, in the course of its physical life. Freed from the limitations and concealments of the physical state, it can now see G-dliness; it can now look back at its own life and experience what it truly was. The soul's experience of the G-dliness it brought into the world with its mitzvot and positive actions is the exquisite pleasure of *Gan Eden* (the "Garden of Eden"—i.e., Paradise); its experience of the destructiveness it wrought through its lapses and transgressions is the excruciating pain of *Gehinom* ("Gehenna" or "Purgatory").

The truth hurts. The truth also cleanses and heals. The spiritual pain of *gehinom*—the soul's pain in facing the truth of its life—cleanses and heals the soul of the spiritual stains and blemishes that its failings and misdeeds have attached to it. Freed of this husk of negativity, the soul is now able to fully enjoy the immeasurable good that its life engendered and "bask in the Divine radiance" emitted by the G-dliness it brought into the world.

For a G-dly soul spawns far more good in its lifetime than evil. The core of the soul is unadulterated goodness; the good we accomplish is infinite, the evil but shallow and superficial. So even the most wicked of souls, say our sages, experiences, at most, twelve months of *gehinom*, followed by an eternity of heaven. Furthermore, a soul's experience of *gehinom* can be mitigated by the action of his or her children and loved ones, here on earth. Reciting Kaddish and engaging in other good deeds "in merit of" and "for the elevation of" the departed soul means that the soul, in effect, is continuing to act positively upon the physical world, thereby adding to the goodness of its physical lifetime.[11]

The soul, on its part, remains involved in the lives of those it leaves behind when it departs physical life. The soul of a parent continues to watch over the lives of his/her children and grandchildren, to derive pride (or pain) from their deeds and accomplishments, and to intercede on their behalf before the Heavenly Throne; the same applies to those to whom a soul was connected with bonds of love, friendship and community. In fact, because the soul is no longer constricted by the limitations of the physical state, its relationship with its loved ones is, in many ways, even deeper and more meaningful than before.

However, while the departed soul is aware and cognizant of all that transpires in the lives of its loved ones, the souls remaining in the physical word are limited to what they can perceive via the five senses as facilitated by their physical bodies. We can impact the soul of a departed loved one through our positive actions, but we cannot communicate with it through conventional means (speech, sight, physical contact, etc.) that, prior to its passing, defined the way that we related to each other. (Indeed, the Torah expressly forbids the idolatrous practices of necromancy, mediumism and similar attempts to "make contact" with the world of the dead.) Hence the occurrence of death, while signifying an elevation for the soul of the departed, is experienced as a tragic loss for those it leaves behind.

Reincarnation: A Second Go

Each individual soul is dispatched to the physical world with its own individualized mission to accomplish. As Jews, we all have the same Torah with the same 613 mitzvot; but each of us has his or her own set of challenges, distinct talents and capabilities, and particular mitzvot which form the crux of his or her mission in life.

At times, a soul may not conclude its mission in a single lifetime. In such cases, it returns to earth for a "second go" to complete the job. This is the concept of *gilgul neshamot*—commonly referred to as "reincarnation"—extensively discussed in the teachings of Kabbalah.[12] This is why we often find ourselves powerfully drawn to a particular mitzvah or cause and make it the focus of our lives, dedicating to it a seemingly disproportionate part of our time and energy: it is our soul gravitating to the "missing pieces" of its Divinely-ordained purpose.[13]

The World to Come

Just as the individual soul passes through three stages—preparation for its mission, the mission itself, and the subsequent phase of satisfaction and reward—so, too, does Creation as a whole. A chain of spiritual "worlds" precede the physical reality, to serve it as a source of Divine vitality and empowerment. Then comes the era of *Olam HaZeh* ("This World") in which the Divine purpose of creation is played out. Finally, once humanity as a whole has completed its mission of making the physical world a "dwelling place for G-d," comes the era of *universal* reward—the World to Come (*Olam HaBa*).

There is a major difference between a soul's individual "world of reward" in *Gan Eden* and the universal reward of the World to Come. Gan Eden is a spiritual world, inhabited by souls without physical bodies; the World to Come is a physical world, inhabited by souls *with* physical bodies[14] (though the very nature of the physical will undergo a fundamental transformation, as per below).

In the World to Come, the physical reality will so perfectly "house" and reflect the Divine reality that it will transcend the finitude and temporality which define it today. Thus, while in today's imperfect world the soul can only experience "reward" after it departs from the body and physical life, in the World to Come, the soul and body will be reunited, and will together enjoy the fruits of their labor. Thus the prophets of Israel spoke of a time when all who died will be restored to life: their bodies will be regenerated[15] and their souls restored to their bodies. "Death will be eradicated forever"[16] and "the world will be filled with the knowledge of G-d as the water covers the sea."[17]

This, of course, will spell the end of the "Era of Achievement."[18] The veil of physicality, rarified to complete transparency, will no longer conceal the truth of G-d, but will rather express it and reveal it in an even more profound way than the most lofty spiritual reality. Goodness and G-dliness will cease to be something we do and achieve, for it will be what we are. Yet our experience of goodness will be absolute. Body and soul both, reunited as they were before they were separated by death, will inhabit all the good that we accomplished with our freely chosen actions in the challenges and concealments of physical life.

FOOTNOTES

1. Ecclesiastes 12:7.
2. See article on chabad.org *Body: The Physical World According to Rabbi Schneur Zalman of Liadi,* and chabad.org articles on *The Purpose of Creation* and *A Dwelling for G-d in the Physical World*
3. Tanya, chapter 6.
4. Talmud, Nidah 30b.
5. Deuteronomy 7:11.
6. Talmud, Eruvin 22a.
7. Ethics of the Fathers 4:17.
8. Thus the Sages speak about a "Gehenna of Fire," in which we experience the full destructive "heat" of our illicit desires, anger and hatreds; and a "Gehenna of Snow," in which we are exposed to the "coldness" of our moments of indifference to G-d and to our fellows.
9. Ethics of the Fathers 3:1; *et al.*
10. Rabbi Israel Baal Shem Tov.
11. This is why there is a greater emphasis on the recitation of Kaddish and other actions for the elevation of a departed soul during the first year after death.
12. Indeed, the Kabbalists say that these days—after 6,000 years of human history—a "new" soul is a rarity; the overwhelming majority of us are reincarnated souls, returned to earth to fill the gaps of a previous lifetime.
13. For more on the subject, see chabad.org articles on *Reincarnation*.
14. This is actually a matter of contention between two great Jewish thinkers and Torah authorities, Maimonides and Nachmanides; the teachings of Kabbalah and Chassidism follow the approach of Nachmonides, who sees the ultimate reward as occurring in a world of embodied souls. For more on this, see chabad.org articles on *The Resurrection of the Dead*.
15. Interestingly, long before the discovery of genetics and the DNA the Talmud talks about a tiny, indestructible bone in the body called *luz* from which the entire body will be "rebuilt" after it returned
16. Isaiah 25:8.
17. Isaiah 11:918. The Talmud goes so far as to quote the verse (Ecclesiastes 12:1), "There will come years of which you will say:

I have no desire in them," and declare: "This refers to the days of the Messianic Era, in which there is neither merit nor obligation" (Talmud, Shabbat 151b).

Judaism and Reincarnation

By **Rabbi Yerachmiel Tilles**

How prevalent is the Jewish belief in reincarnation today? How does it differ from the Asian belief? What do the Rabbis think of it?

The root of the word "Torah" is the verb "to instruct". Torah's primary function is to teach us how to live Jewishly, in harmony with G-d's will. As such, the basic levels of scriptural interpretation lead to a *practical* understanding of mitzvot and related Jewish values.

The Torah, however, is a multilayered document. Many of its deeper levels of interpretation are not readily accessible; and they may not lend themselves to obvious, practical application in daily life. As such, these more esoteric aspects of Torah are not of interest to significant segments of the Jewish population, including some rabbis and scholars.

Consequently, many Jews are surprised to learn, or may even wish to deny, that reincarnation—the "revolving" of souls through a succession of lives, or *"gilgulim"*— is an integral part of Jewish belief. But this teaching has always been around. And it is firmly rooted in source-verses.

Examples abound. Ramban, one of the greatest commentators on the Torah (and on the Talmud), and a seminal figure in Jewish history, hints several times that reincarnation is the key to penetrating the deep mysteries involved in the mitzvah of *yibum* (the obligation of the brother of a childless, deceased man to marry the widow). In his explanation of Gen. 38:8, he insists that Yehudah and his sons were aware of the secret of reincarnation, and that this was a major factor in their respective attitudes towards Tamar.

The Jewish understanding of reincarnation is different from Buddhist doctrines. It in no way leads to fatalism. At every point of *moral* decision in his life, a Jew has complete free choice. If not for freedom of choice, how unfair it would be of G-d to make demands of us—especially when reward and punishment is involved! Reincarnation does not imply pre-determination. It is, rather, an opportunity for rectification and soul-perfection.

The holy Ari explained it most simply: every Jew must fulfill all 613 mitzvot, and if he doesn't succeed in one lifetime, he comes back again and again until he finishes. For this reason, events in a person's life may lead him towards certain places, encounters, etc., in ways that may or may not make sense. Divine providence provides each person with the *opportunities* he needs to fulfill those particular mitzvot necessary for the perfection of his soul. But the *responsibility* lies with us. At the actual moment of decision in any given situation, the choice is ours.

One of the ways in which heaven maintains our ability to exercise complete freedom of choice is by not allowing us conscious knowledge of previous incarnations. Consequently, it might seem to some people that there is little *practical* benefit in being aware of this doctrine. Furthermore, many scholars contend that these mystical concepts can easily be misunderstood, or carried to erroneous and misleading conclusions. We can therefore understand why this and similar subjects are only hinted at in scripture, and why some knowledge and a great deal of determination are often required in order to gain access to this information.

For an in-depth English treatment of the Jewish doctrine of reincarnation, see the running translation and commentary of *Shaar Gilgulim* on KabbalaOnline.org. The English edition of *"Derech Hashem,"* by Rabbi Moshe-Chaim Luzzatto, "The Way of G-d", translated by Aryeh Kaplan (Feldheim, 1983), II:3:10 (page 125) plus notes 39-40 (pp. 342-3) provides an English list of Torah sources on this topic in both scripture and Kabbalah.

In Which Body Will a Reincarnated Soul Return?

By **Rabbi Dovid Zaklikowski**

Question:

If a soul is reincarnated in different bodies, in which one does it return to in the time of Moshiach?

Answer:

Great question.

First, though, we need to explain why a soul is reincarnated into another body in the first place.

A soul is reincarnated when it did not accomplish all of its obligations during its stay in a specific body. The person may have completed his particular mission on this world; however the soul has to complete all of the 613 commandments in order to achieve completion for all of its 613 components. Thus the soul descends once again to finish the task.

Every body which was inhabited by the soul assisted the soul in the fulfillment of its mission. Those components of the soul which were rectified through the mitzvot fulfilled by a particular body always maintain a connection with that body, and will return to that body to revive it with the Resurrection of the Dead. In short this means that souls will be divided into different bodies.

How is that possible, you may be wondering? The Divine soul is a reflection of its infinite source, G-d Himself, and thus has the ability to vivify any number of bodies. In fact, according to the mystics' teachings, the entire soul of a person is never "clothed" in its body. Only a ray of the soul descends into the body, for otherwise the body would be completely overwhelmed by the soul's brilliant intensity.

Lesson 5
Eternal Bond

יִתְגַּדֵּל וְיִתְקַדַּשׁ שְׁמֵהּ רַבָּא

Introduction

What happens to the love we feel for our loved ones once they are gone? Does the relationship stop short? Or are there ways in which we can continue to meaningfully connect with those who have passed on?

In Lesson Five, we will learn that, although the means of communication shift, we can continue to relate to the souls of the departed. We will learn of many ways to give our gift of love to them, and also how they continue to share of themselves with us.

A Shifting Relationship

Text 1a

וְעַל כָּרְחֲךָ אַתָּה חַי

משנה אבות ד,כב

Against your will, you must live.

MISHNAH, AVOT 4:22

Text 1b

יָפָה שָׁעָה אַחַת בִּתְשׁוּבָה וּמַעֲשִׂים טוֹבִים בָּעוֹלָם הַזֶּה מִכָּל חַיֵּי הָעוֹלָם הַבָּא

משנה אבות ד,יז

One hour of *teshuvah* [repentance; lit., *return*] and good deeds in this world is better than the entire life of the world to come.

IBID., 4:17

Text 1c

וְעַל כׇּרְחֲךָ אַתָּה מֵת

משנה אבות ה,כב

And against your will you must die.

IBID., 4:22

The Bond with the Beyond
Many Ways to Connect

Text 2

When the child says Kaddish for his father or mother, it is like sending regards. When he learns a chapter of Mishnah on their behalf, it is like sending them a letter. And when he fulfills mitzvot and good deeds for the benefit of their souls, it is like sending them an entire package.

RABBI GAVRIEL ZINNER, NITEI GAVRIEL, LAWS OF MOURNING II

Rabbi Gavriel Zinner. Rabbi and prolific author; leads a congregation in Boro Park, Brooklyn. Renowned for his authorship of the multivolume *Nitei Gavriel,* which collects relevant *halachic* material divided by topic. In addition, the work includes the varied customs prevalent in different communities, and is widely used because of Zinner's concise and lucid language and easy accessibility.

Kaddish

Text 3

יִתְגַּדַּל וְיִתְקַדַּשׁ שְׁמֵהּ רַבָּא

בְּעָלְמָא דִּי בְרָא כִרְעוּתֵהּ וְיַמְלִיךְ מַלְכוּתֵהּ

וְיַצְמַח פּוּרְקָנֵהּ וִיקָרֵב מְשִׁיחֵיהּ

בְּחַיֵּיכוֹן וּבְיוֹמֵיכוֹן וּבְחַיֵּי דְכָל בֵּית יִשְׂרָאֵל

בַּעֲגָלָא וּבִזְמַן קָרִיב. וְאִמְרוּ אָמֵן

יְהֵא שְׁמֵהּ רַבָּא מְבָרַךְ לְעָלַם וּלְעָלְמֵי עָלְמַיָּא

יִתְבָּרַךְ וְיִשְׁתַּבַּח וְיִתְפָּאַר וְיִתְרוֹמַם וְיִתְנַשֵּׂא

וְיִתְהַדָּר וְיִתְעַלֶּה וְיִתְהַלָּל שְׁמֵהּ דְּקֻדְשָׁא בְּרִיךְ הוּא

לְעֵלָּא מִן כָּל בִּרְכָתָא וְשִׁירָתָא

תֻּשְׁבְּחָתָא וְנֶחֱמָתָא

דַּאֲמִירָן בְּעָלְמָא. וְאִמְרוּ אָמֵן

[יְהֵא שְׁלָמָא רַבָּא מִן שְׁמַיָּא

וְחַיִּים טוֹבִים עָלֵינוּ וְעַל כָּל יִשְׂרָאֵל. וְאִמְרוּ אָמֵן:

עֹשֶׂה שָׁלוֹם בִּמְרוֹמָיו הוּא יַעֲשֶׂה שָׁלוֹם עָלֵינוּ

וְעַל כָּל יִשְׂרָאֵל. וְאִמְרוּ אָמֵן]

סידור נוסח האריז״ל, קדיש

Yitgadal ve'yitkadash shemei raba . . . .

May He establish His kingship, give blossom to His redemption, and hasten [the coming of] His Messiah in your lifetime and in your days, and in the lifetime of the entire House of Israel, speedily and soon. And say: Amen.

May His great Name be blessed forever and to all eternity.

Blessed and praised, glorified, exalted and extolled, honored, upraised, and lauded be the Name of the Holy One, Blessed be He, beyond all the blessings and songs, praises, and consolations that are uttered in the world.

And say: Amen . . . .

Siddur, Nusach HaAriZal, Kaddish

Text 4

Although only the body of the child comes from the parents, not the soul, still, the soul enters this world as a result of the parents' choice to have children. Therefore, when the child is righteous and serves G-d, it is on account of the parents who brought the child into the world. This was the reason for Abraham's strong desire to have a child—not in order to have an heir to inherit his wealth, but for the abovementioned purpose. This is the greatest merit [parents can have]: leaving offspring in the world who can serve G-d, which in turn is like the deceased themselves remaining alive and continuing to serve G-d, since they gave birth to these children.

Rabbi Shlomo ben Aderet, Responsa, Volume 5, Number 48

Rabbi Shlomo ben Aderet (1235–1310). Also known by the acronym Rashba; Born in Barcelona, Spain; premier student of Nachmanides; leader of Spanish Jewry; medieval rabbi and Talmudist; authority on Jewish law. More than 3,000 of his *responsa* are extant. The Rashba was drawn into the controversy over the writings of Maimonides. Despite his reservations about some of Maimonides' philosophic teachings, he defended the *Mishneh Torah* and *Guide for the Perplexed*. Among his numerous students were the Ritva, Rabbeinu Bachaye, and the Re'ah.

Text 5

Rabbi Akiva once saw a man, darkened by coal dust, carrying an extremely heavy load of firewood on his head and running at a rapid pace. Rabbi Akiva commanded the man to stop.

Rabbi Akiva said to him, "Why are you running with such a heavy load? If you are a slave, I shall free you! If you are poor and must exert yourself to such an inhuman extent, let me give you money and make you wealthy!"

"Please," the man entreated Rabbi Akiva, "Let me continue my work, lest my overseers become angry with me!"

Rabbi Akiva asked, "And what is your work?"

The man replied, "I am the soul of a dead man. Each day, I am sent to collect wood for a giant fire into which I am then cast."

Rabbi Akiva asked, "What was your occupation in this world?"

The man answered, "I was a tax collector. I took bribes from the rich, and I had the poor executed."

Rabbi Akiva inquired, "My son, have you not heard in the other worlds that something might be done to help you and alleviate your suffering?"

"Please," he cried, "Allow me to resume my work. My task-masters will be angry with me and punish me further. They say that I have no way of being redeemed. Had I had a child who would stand up in public and cause others to praise G-d through prayers or Kaddish, then they could release me from this punishment. But I left a wife who was pregnant . . . and there is no one who would teach my child Torah, for I have no friend left in the world."

At that moment, Rabbi Akiva resolved to seek out and teach this man's child.

"What is your name?"

"My name is Akiva, my wife's name is Shoshniba, and I am from the town of Ludkiya," said the man.

Rabbi Akiva felt extremely pained because of this soul and he traveled until he came to that very town. He asked, "Where is this man's house?"

The villagers answered in hatred, "May his bones be ground to dust in hell!"

"Where is this man's wife?"

The villagers answered with bitterness, "May her name and memory be blotted out from this world!"

"Where is this man's child?"

"He is uncircumcised, and no one will circumcise him!"

Rabbi Akiva took the man's son, circumcised him, and began to teach him Torah. But the boy would not accept his teaching. Rabbi Akiva fasted for forty days on his behalf until a heavenly voice said, "Rabbi Akiva, you may [now] teach him."

Rabbi Akiva taught him Torah, and to recite the *shema*, silent prayer, and grace after meals. He placed the child

Rabbi Yitschak ben Moshe of Vienna (ca. 1180–1250). Student of the German Tosafists. His fame comes from his halachic work and commentary to the Talmud, *Or Zarua*. This work was subsequently quoted by many halachic authorities and is influential in Jewish law. His son, Rabbi Chaim, wrote a compendium of his father's work, which for many generations was the only widely used version of the *Or Zarua*. In the 19th century, the original work was found and published. Among his students was the Maharam of Rothenburg.

before the congregation, and he lead them in prayers and in the reciting of Kaddish.

Then the soul was spared from his punishment. He came to Rabbi Akiva in a dream and said, "May G-d grant you a portion in Heaven because you have spared me from the punishments of hell."

. . . . From here we learn that when a child recites Kaddish, he spares his father from punishment.

RABBI YITSCHAK BEN MOSHE OF VIENNA,
OR ZARUA II, LAWS OF SHABBAT, CHAPTER 50

Torah Study

Text 6

Even greater than reciting Kaddish for the sake of their souls is the study of the holy Torah. This extricates them from all chambers of *Gehinnom*, and illuminates a path upon which they can proceed to *Gan Eden* . . . . there is no other mitzvah which compares to the study of the holy Torah . . . particularly the study of Mishnah.

NITEI GAVRIEL, LAWS OF MOURNING II, OP. CIT.

Yizkor and Charity

Text 7

יִזְכּוֹר אֱלֹקִים נִשְׁמַת אָבִי מוֹרִי (פלוני בר פלונית)

שֶׁהָלַךְ לְעוֹלָמוֹ

בַּעֲבוּר שֶׁאֲנִי נוֹדֵר צְדָקָה בַּעֲדוֹ

וּבִשְׂכַר זֶה תְּהֵא נַפְשׁוֹ צְרוּרָה בִּצְרוֹר הַחַיִּים

עִם נִשְׁמַת אַבְרָהָם יִצְחָק וְיַעֲקֹב שָׂרָה רִבְקָה רָחֵל וְלֵאָה

וְעִם שְׁאָר צַדִּיקִים וְצִדְקָנִיּוֹת שֶׁבְּגַן עֵדֶן וְנֹאמַר אָמֵן

סידור נוסח האריז״ל, תפילת שחרית ליום טוב

May G-d remember the soul of my father/ mother, my teacher (mention the Hebrew name and that of the mother) who has gone to his/her [supernal] world, because I will—without obligating myself with a vow—donate charity for his/her sake. In this merit, may his/her soul be bound up in the bond of life with the souls of Abraham, Isaac, and Jacob, Sarah, Rebecca, Rachel, and Leah, and with the other righteous men and women who are in *Gan Eden*; and let us say, Amen.

Siddur, Nusach HaAriZal, Festival Morning Prayers

Rabbi Mordechai ben Hillel (ca. 1240–1298). Renowned codifier, author, and martyr; a devout student of the Maharam of Rothenburg. His work, referred to as the *Mordechai,* is a collection of tosafot, *responsa*, quotes from various other sages, and halachic decisions. This work had a major influence on Talmudic scholarship, and is printed in the back of most editions of the Talmud. He, along with his wife—the daughter of Rabbi Yechiel of Paris—and their five children, were killed during a massacre in Nuremburg, Germany in 1298.

Text 8a

We are accustomed to pledge charity on behalf of the deceased on Yom Kippur, for the deceased require forgiveness.

RABBI MORDECHAI BEN HILLEL, MORDECHAI, YOMA 1:727

Rabbi Eliezer ben Yehudah of Worms (ca. 1160–1230). Rabbi, yeshivah head, and kabbalist; author and liturgical poet. Student of Rabbi Eliezer of Metz (author of *Sefer Yerei'im*) and Rabbi Yehudah HaChasid (leader of the mystic group *Chasidei Ashkenaz).* Rabbi Eliezer wrote on Halachah, Kabbalah and the *siddur,* but is best known for his halachic work titled *Sefer Rokeach.* His wife and son were killed during one of the massacres committed during the Crusades.

Text 8b

After we pledge charity on behalf of the deceased on Yom Kippur, how does it help the deceased once the living give that charity on their behalf?

G-d examines the hearts of the living and the dead and can see if the dead would have wanted to give charity themselves, and if they were poor, that they were good of heart. . . .

RABBI ELAZAR BEN YEHUDAH OF WORMS,
SEFER ROKEACH, LAWS OF YOM KIPPUR, CHAPTER 217

And the Living Shall Take to Heart

Learning Activity 1

Write your answers to these questions in your book. Be prepared to defend your answer when asked.

Would you rather go to a wedding or to a funeral? Why?

Which of the two is the more meaningful and spiritual experience? Why?

Text 9 📖

טוֹב לָלֶכֶת אֶל בֵּית אֵבֶל מִלֶּכֶת אֶל בֵּית מִשְׁתֶּה בַּאֲשֶׁר הוּא סוֹף כָּל הָאָדָם וְהַחַי יִתֵּן אֶל לִבּוֹ

קהלת ז,ב

t is better to go to the house of mourning, than to go to the house of feasting; for that is the end of all men; and the living will take it to heart.

KOHELET/ECCLESIASTES 7:2

Text 10 📖

Rabbi Moshe ben Maimon (1135–1204). Better known as Maimonides or by the acronym Rambam. Born in Córdoba, Spain. After the conquest of Córdoba by the Almohads, who sought to forcibly convert the Jews to Islam, he fled and eventually settled in Cairo. There he became the leader of the Jewish community and served as court physician to the vizier of Egypt. His rulings on Jewish law are considered integral to the formation of halachic consensus. He is most noted for authoring the *Mishneh Torah*, an encyclopedic arrangement of Jewish law. His philosophical work, *Guide for the Perplexed*, is also well-known.

כל מי שאינו מתאבל כמו שצוו חכמים הרי זה אכזרי, אלא יפחד וידאג ויפשפש במעשיו ויחזור בתשובה

משנה תורה הלכות אבל יג,יב

ne who does not mourn as prescribed by our sages is a callous individual. Rather, a mourner should be anxious and concerned, and evaluate his behavior and repent.

RAMBAM, MISHNEH TORAH, LAWS OF MOURNING 13:12

Text 11

One might argue that after the soul has risen and elevated, rising level above spiritual level, it no longer desires to descend and return to the lower corporeal worlds. By its very nature the soul desires only to rise.

However, the truth is that an ascent in and of itself is not yet perfection . . . . From the sublimation and elevation there must be an influence below . . . .

The soul actually desires and yearns that through its spiritual elevation there will be an increase of good acts in the lower worlds. This includes those good deeds, Torah, prayer, and charity that are performed for the sake of bringing an elevation to the soul.

In general, we speak of the principle that "the living must take to heart (Kohelet/Ecclesiastes 7:2)," in order for the resulting actions on the part of the living to bring not only elevation to the soul in the supernal worlds, but also for the influence that it has on the lower worlds.

RABBI MENACHEM MENDEL SCHNEERSON,
SEFER HASICHOT 5749 , VOLUME I, PAGE 232

Rabbi Menachem Mendel Schneerson (1902–1994). Known as "the Lubavitcher Rebbe," or simply as "the Rebbe." Born in southern Ukraine. Rabbi Schneerson escaped from the Nazis, arriving in the US in June 1941. The towering Jewish leader of the twentieth century, the Rebbe inspired and guided the revival of traditional Judaism after the European devastation, and often emphasized that the performance of just one additional good deed could usher in the era of Mashiach.

Yahrtzeit

Text 12 📖

כנודע שכל עמל האדם שעמלה נפשו בחייו למעלה בבחי׳ העלם והסתר
מתגלה ומאיר בבחי׳ גילוי מלמעלה למטה בעת פטירתו

תניא, אגרת הקודש כח

Rabbi Shne'ur Zalman of Liadi (1745–1812). Known as "the Alter Rebbe" and "the Rav"; Born in Liozna, Belarus; buried in Hadiach, Ukraine; chassidic Rebbe and founder of the Chabad movement; among the principal students of the Magid of Mezeritch. His numerous works include the *Tanya,* an early classic of Chassidism; *Torah Or* and *Likutei Torah*; and *Shulchan Aruch HaRav,* a rewritten code of Jewish law. He was succeeded by his son, Rabbi Dovber of Lubavitch.

For as is known, all the effort of man, in which his soul toiled during his lifetime, [and which remains] above in a hidden and concealed state, is revealed and radiates in a manifest way, from above downwards, at the time of his passing.

RABBI SHNE'UR ZALMAN OF LIADI, TANYA, IGERET HAKODESH 28

Text 13 📖

A yahrtzeit is generally associated with two mixed feelings. On one hand, we learn from our sages that the soul of the departed rises from one spiritual world to a higher one. This is, therefore, a day of rejoicing for the soul, hence a day of corresponding joy for the near and dear ones left behind. On the other hand, the *yahrtzeit* naturally emphasizes the loss sustained by the family, which results in a feeling of sadness. In truth, however, the *yahrtzeit* should not call forth feelings of sadness, but rather, a feeling of reflection, self-examination, and repentance.

During this day, one should work to align one's life on this earth with the path followed by the soul above, which is constantly on the ascent. This is to say, just as the soul continuously rises year after year, going from strength to strength, so must those associated with the soul steadily rise in their advancement in Torah knowledge and observance of mitzvot. By doing so, they give the soul of the departed the greatest possible joy.

This approach underlines the basic view of Judaism that, in reality, there is no "death" in matters of G-dliness. Rather, the *yahrtzeit*, and even the very day of passing, represents a transition. But this transition is unique for it goes in only one direction—higher and higher, from strength to strength—first in this world, and later in the following world.

RABBI MENACHEM MENDEL SCHNEERSON,
FROM A MESSAGE TO A YAHRTZEIT GATHERING, 1952

Visiting the Gravesite

Text 14

תלת שמהן אקרי נשמתא דבר נש נפש רוחא ונשמתא . . . נפש דא אשתכחת
גו קברא . . . ובדא מתגלגלת בהאי עלמא לאשתכחא גו חייא ולמנדע
בצערא דלהון ובשעתא די אצטריכו בעאת רחמי עלייהו . . . וכד אצטריך
לבני עלמא כד אינון בצערא ואזלי לבי קברי האי נפש אתערת ואיהי אזלא
ומשטטא ואתערת לרוח וההוא רוח אתער לגבי אבהן וסליק ואתער לגבי
נשמה וכדין קודשא בריך הוא חייס על עלמא והא אוקימנא

זוהר ב קמא,ב

The soul of man is called by three names: *nefesh,
ruach,* and *neshamah* . . . . The *nefesh* is present
in the grave . . . and it roams this world to be
among the living and to be acquainted with their pain.
At a time of need, it pleads for mercy for them . . . .

And when the inhabitants of the world are in need,
when they are in sorrow and they go to the cemetery,
the *nefesh* awakens. It goes and floats and awakens *ruach,*
and the *ruach* is awakened at the place of the Patriarchs.
It ascends and arouses the *neshamah.* Then the Holy
One, blessed be He, has mercy on the world as we have
already established.

RABBI SHIMON BAR YOCHAI, ZOHAR II,141B

Rabbi Shimon bar Yochai (2nd century CE). Known by the acronym Rashbi; scholar of the Mishnah and founder of Jewish mysticism; an eminent disciple of Rabbi Akiva. The kabbalistic classic *Sefer HaZohar* is attributed to him and his disciples. Because of the Roman persecutions he was forced to hide with his son Eliezer for 13 years. Lag Ba'Omer is commemorated as the day of his passing, with thousands visiting his grave in Meron, Israel.

The *Ohel:* An Overview (Optional Section)

Text 15

When there are wise and pious people of a generation who had the merit of receiving the Divine spirit upon them, through them the rest of the people of the generation can also benefit from that supernal spirit .... this is not only true in the lives of these lofty individuals, but even when they have passed on. This lofty spirit is to be found at their gravesites, for their very bones were the vessels upon which this lofty spirit rested. And some of this remains, enough to benefit those that avail themselves of it.

RABBI NISSIM BEN REUVEN, DERASHOT HARAN, EIGHTH HOMILY

Rabbi Nissim ben Reuven of Gerona (1320–1380). Known by the acronym Ran; influential Talmudist and authority on Jewish law; among the last great Spanish Talmudic scholars. Considered the outstanding halachic authority of his generation, queries came to him from throughout the Diaspora. His works include commentaries on the Talmud and on Rabbi Yitschak Alfasi's code, *responsa* literature, a commentary on the Bible, and a collection of sermons, *Derashot HaRan*, which elucidates fundamentals of Judaism.

G-d's Candle

Text 16

נשמתהון דישראל אתגזרו מגו בוצינא קדישא דדליק דכתיב (משלי כ,כז)
"נר ה' נשמת אדם" והאי נר בשעתא דאתאחד מגו אורייתא דלעילא לא
שכיך נהורא עליה אפילו רגעא . . . נהורא דשרגא כיון דאתאחדא גו פתילה
ההוא נהורא לא שכיך לעלמין אלא מתנענעא נהורא לכאן ולכאן ולא
משתכיך לעלמין, כגוונא דא ישראל דנשמתייהו מגו ההוא נהורא דשרגא
כיון דאמר מלה חדא דאורייתא הא נהורא דליק ולא יכלון אינון לאשתככא
ומתנענען לכאן ולכאן ולכל סטרין כנהורא דשרגא

זוהר ג ריח,ב

The souls of Israel have been hewn from the Holy Lamp, as is written, "The spirit of Man is the lamp of the Lord (Mishlei/Proverbs 20:27)." Now once this lamp has been kindled from the supernal Torah, the light upon it never ceases for an instant, like the flame of a wick which is never still for an instant. So when an Israelite has said one word of the Torah, a light is kindled and he cannot keep still, but sways to and fro like the flame of a wick.

ZOHAR, OP. CIT., III, 218B

Text 17

The soul is hewn from the light of the Divine Intellect, and therefore the soul experiences enormous joy in the presence of light. The soul is drawn toward light for both are of the same species, albeit one is physical and one is spiritual, pure and uncompounded. This is why King Solomon wrote: "The spirit of Man is the lamp of the Lord (Proverbs 20:27)."

RABBEINU BACHAYE, TERUMAH 25:31

Rabbeinu Bachaye ben Asher (ca. 1255–1340). Renowned Spanish biblical exegete, born at Saragossa, Spain; a pupil of the Rashba. His work on the Torah combines different styles of understanding, including a kabbalistic approach. He also authored a work on ethics, *Kad HaKemach.*

Key Points

1. The soul descends to this world for the ability to perform mitzvot.

2. After a body departs from this world, its soul can no longer perform mitzvot, but the living can perform mitzvot on that soul's behalf.

3. Our actions on behalf of the departed elevate the soul, bring us blessings, and most importantly allow that soul to live on through us.

4. We must also focus on ourselves, using times of mourning and yahrtzeits to inspire us to improve, grow, and live more meaningful lives.

5. Times of passing and yahrtzeits have a positive, joyous element—the soul completes its life mission, and its light shines forth brighter and brighter.

6. Even after departing, the soul remains connected and interested in the world. It will pray for us, and our good deeds bring it immeasurable satisfaction.

7. There are many customs and practices centered on this theme of the continued relationship between the living and the departed.

8. The relationship between souls, especially loved ones, is everlasting. The living and the departed continue to help each other.

Additional Readings

Death and Grieving

By **Rabbi Simon Jacobson**

And the living shall take to heart—Ecclesiastes, 7:2

The soul never dies—The Rebbe

In 1950, after the passing of his predecessor and father-in-law, the Rebbe emphasized that it was important not to eulogize the deceased, but to let their good deeds speak for them. Citing a letter that his father-in-law wrote in 1920, after the passing of his own father, the Rebbe explained that a true leader is like a shepherd who never abandons his flock, leaving behind a philosophy and a clear course of action. Indeed, he explained, "he is even more present than during his lifetime, since his soul is freed from the physical constraints of time and space."

What Does Death Really Mean?

Death: The very word strikes fear in people's hearts. They consider death as unfathomable as it is inevitable. They are barely able to talk about it, to peer beyond the word itself and allow themselves to contemplate its true implications. This is an understandable reaction, given the fact that so many people think of *life* as nothing more than a state in which the human body is biologically active. But it is time to ask ourselves: What happens after death, if anything? What does death really mean? How should the surviving loved ones react?

The mystery of death is part of the enigma of the soul and of life itself; understanding death really means understanding life. During life as we know it, the body is vitalized by the soul; upon death, there is a separation between body and soul. But the soul continues to live on as it always has, now unfettered by the physical constraints of the body. And since a person's true

character—his goodness, virtue, and selflessness—lies in the soul, it is logical to assume that he will ascend to a higher state after fulfilling his responsibilities on Earth.

Modern physics has taught us that no substance truly disappears, that it only changes form. A tree, for instance, might be cut down and used to build a house, or a table, or a chair. Regardless of how the form changes, the wood remains wood. And when that same wood is burned in a furnace, it again changes form, becoming an energy that gives off heat and gas. The tree, the chair, and the fire are all merely different forms of the same substance.

If this is the case with a material substance, it is even more so with a spiritual substance. The spiritual life force in man, the soul, never disappears; upon death, it simply changes from one form to another, higher form. This may be difficult to comprehend at first, since we are so dependent on using our sensory tools to get through life. With wood, for example, it is easier to hold a chair in our hands than to hold fire; and yet, anyone who has ever seen or felt a fire cannot doubt for a moment that it exists.

No matter what physical ailments might befall a person, they are just that: *physical* ailments. Nothing that happens to the flesh and blood diminishes in any way the soul's power, which is purely spiritual. It is inappropriate, therefore, to use the term "afterlife" to define what happens after death. "Afterlife" implies that we have entered another, separate place, whereas death is actually a continuation of life as we know it, only in a new, higher form. The chapter in Genesis discussing the death of Sarah, for instance, is called "The Life of Sarah." The chapter discussing the death of Jacob is called "And Jacob Lived." How odd it now seems to name death "Life"!

So before we can truly answer the question "What is death?" we must first ask, "What is life?" By medical definition, life takes place when one's brain and heart are functioning. Yet a person can be biologically alive but not alive at all; breathing and walking and talking are only the *manifestations* of what we call life. The true source of life, the energy that allows the body to function, is the soul. And the soul, because it is connected to G-d, the giver of life, is immortal. While the manifestations of life may cease upon death, the soul lives on, only in a different form.

How can a mortal human being connect to eternal life? By living a material life that fuses body and soul, thereby connecting to G-d. A person who transforms his or her body into a vehicle for love and generosity is a person who nurtures his or her eternal soul. It is by giving life to others that one becomes truly alive.

To a person for whom life consists of material gains, death indeed represents the end. It is the time when fleeting achievements come to a halt. But to a person for whom life consists of spiritual gains, life never ends. The soul is fueled by the inexhaustible energy of the good deeds a person performed on Earth, and it lives on materially through his or her children and the others who perpetuate his or her spiritual vitality. As the sages say, "Just as his descendants are alive, he, too, is alive."

We often have a hard time distinguishing between biological life and spiritual life, or true life. We are distracted by the many material trappings of biological life. Once the soul leaves the body, though, we can clearly see how it lives on, how that soul inspires people to perform good deeds, to educate and help others, to live G-dly and spiritual lives. It is when a righteous person physically departs the Earth that he or she begins to exert the most profound influence.

A revered and aged rabbi, when he was very near death, asked that he be moved into the study hall where he delivered his discourses. "Soon I am going to Heaven," he told his followers, "but I am leaving you all my writings, and along with them, my spirit."

When his grandson heard these words, he began to weep. His grandfather, weak with illness, turned to him and said, "Emotions? Emotions? No. Intellect, intellect." From that moment on, the boy thought only of the life of his grandfather's soul, not the death of his body.

What Does Death Mean for the Survivors?

While death represents the soul's elevation to a higher level, it nevertheless remains a painful experience for the survivors. At the same time, it must serve—as must all experiences in life—as a lesson. We must see death not as a negative force, but as an opportunity for growth.

Since death provokes such strong emotions, we must have a clear channel through which to express them, to go about healing in a constructive way. When a loved one dies, two powerful and conflicting emotions are aroused: sadness over the loss and confusion about the future. The sages teach us that it would be barbaric not to mourn at all, but that we should not mourn longer than necessary. A week of mourning is sufficient; otherwise, a person's death becomes a presence unto itself, continuously saddening us and impeding our progress in life.

But why should we restrain our natural pain and sadness over a loved one's death? Grief is a feeling, after all, and feelings cannot be controlled, can they? Isn't it wrong to set limits on our grief, or to try to channel it in a certain direction?

True, feelings are feelings, but we *can* choose whether to experience them in a destructive or productive light. The key in this case is to understand death for what it is, to celebrate its positive element: A mourner must realize that the soul of his or her loved one has now reached an even greater place than it occupied during its time on Earth, and that it will continue to rise. It is the act of reconciling this positive realization against our grief that can turn death from a traumatic experience into a cathartic one.

To diminish our expression of grief is unhealthy and inappropriate, but to allow our grief to overwhelm us is to selfishly overlook the true meaning of death—the fact that a righteous person's soul has found an even more righteous home.

Because the strongest bond between a mother and daughter or a husband and wife is a spiritual one, it remains strong after death. Mourning also helps us retain this bond, for the soul of a departed person, eternal and intact, watches over the people with whom she was close. Every gracious act gives her great pleasure and satisfaction, particularly when such acts are committed in a manner that she taught, whether by instruction or example.

Her soul is fully aware of what is happening to the friends and relatives she has left behind. The soul is distressed when they experience undue grief or depression, and it rejoices when they move beyond their initial pain and continue to build their lives and inspire those around them.

There is no way to replace a departed loved one, for each person is a complete world. But there is a way to help fill the void. When family and friends supplement their customary good deeds with further virtuous acts on behalf of the departed, they continue the work of his or her soul. By performing such acts in the memory of a loved one, we can truly build a living memorial.

But after all is said and done, death can be an incomprehensible, devastating experience to those who are left behind. After all the rationalizations, all the explanations, the heart still cries. And it *should* cry.

When a friend or relative is grieving for a loved one, do not try to explain; just be there with them. Soothe and console them, and weep with them. There is nothing you can really say, for no matter how we might try, we must accept that we often do not understand G-d's mysterious ways.

Ask of G-d to finally bring the day when death shall be no more, when "death shall be swallowed up forever and G-d shall wipe the tears from every face" (Isaiah 25:8).

This is an excerpt from *Toward a Meaningful Life – The Wisdom of the Rebbe* by Rabbi Simon Jacobson.

Yisroel
As told to **Rochel Yaffe**

It was five-thirty on a Monday afternoon, and my classroom was still at last, a deserted battlefield. The radiators and window were still covered with odd socks and mittens—it had been a snowy winter. The room was littered with worksheets, economically converted into paper airplanes. The children made no pretense of taking their test papers home. Their parents couldn't read them, they told me candidly, and didn't care much about Hebrew School anyway. And that's what it was, I reflected wearily, a battle for two hours a day, between myself—"The Rabbi"—and fifteen restless twelve-year-olds who could see no purpose in what I was trying to teach them.

They were not bad children, for the most part. Only a few were insolent or rebellious. But they were all . . . indifferent. They came straggling in reluctantly every day, chattering about expensive presents they had received for Chanukah or were planning to get for their birthdays, about skiing trips and vacations in Florida. They sat before me and spoke, in their innocence, their ignorance, of lobster and Chinese food, of basketball on Shabbat morning (in the Jewish Center of course) and movies on Shabbat afternoon. And when I finally silenced them to begin *Modeh Ani,* I wondered if too much had already happened to these children since they had opened their eyes on G-d's world, if it was too late in the day to acknowledge the living and eternal King.

I spoke of my frustrations, as teachers do, to Mr. Gruber, veteran of fifteen years at the school. "Let me give you some advice," he told me. "Don't beat your head against a stone wall. This is not New York, remember, it's Lowell—*Lo Kel*, the place without a G-d. It's no use. Believe me, I tried, for years. Give them a good show for the Bar Mitzvah. It's all they care about."

When I repeated this conversation to Miriam—in the two years we had lived out-of-town she had become my friend as well as my wife—she was angry. Mr. Gruber might be bitter and discouraged, but that was no excuse for us. We, who had grown up in 770, near the Rebbe, in the strong bright light of his love for every Jew, how could we give up on any Jew, especially a Jewish child? She was right, I knew. The spark was there, waiting. If only I knew how to ignite it, how to open their minds, their hearts. I didn't expect great things, not any more. "Open for me the eye of a needle . . . "

At that moment, as if on cue, the door opened. Yisroel Levine stood in the doorway, cheeks and nose bright red from the cold, snow crusting his thick brown bangs. "My mother is still not here, and I'm frozen. Can I wait inside?"

"Sure. Come on in and thaw out."

I liked Yisroel, a slight, agile boy, with lively grey eyes and a quick smile. His father came to shul once in a while for a *yahrzeit*, and we had become acquainted. A graying doctor with a bad heart, he spoke sardonically of his strictly orthodox childhood, but admitted he wanted Yisroel to know more than his older brothers, who were growing up to be "*gantze goyim*," as he put it. When it was his turn to pick up Yisroel, he usually stopped for a chat. Perhaps because of the small bond this established between us, Yisroel gave me little trouble, and even took my part sometimes with a "Shut—up—you—guys—the—Rabbi -is—waiting."

Now he looked around the room and said sympathetically, "Wow, this place is a mess." He tossed his ski jacket in a corner. "Want me to help clean up?"

"Sure, Yisroel," I teased. "You can begin by picking up that jacket. And check the radiator. I think half the mittens are yours."

"Rabbi, may I speak to you alone for a moment?" Marsha, the school secretary spoke quietly, but something in her voice caused me to stride down the hail to her office, my heart racing with fear. Miriam? I wondered. The baby? He had been feverish all night. There had indeed been a tragedy, I discovered, but found, with guilty relief, that it was not my own. Yisroel's mother would not be here to pick him up. Her car had skidded in the snow and hit a tree. She had died before the ambulance arrived. I was to take Yisroel home, saying only that his mother had been delayed. His father would break the news to the children when he returned from the hospital.

All the way home, riding through the lovely snow-covered New England streets, Yisroel chattered on. He said that recesses should be longer, and *davening* shorter, and that once a week was more than enough of Hebrew School. He must have thought I agreed with everything, because I could only nod silently, struck dumb by what I knew awaited the child when he arrived home.

At last we stopped by the neat white frame house with its green shutters. Yisroel, thoughtless, oblivious, jumped out, called, "Thanks, Rabbi. See you on Wednesday, unless there is a snowstorm." He bent to scoop up a handful of snow, and tossed a snowball lightly at my rear window. That carefree gesture haunted me during the days that followed. It was the last time, I knew, that I would see Yisroel in his untouched childhood.

Two days later, I was walking up the well-shoveled steps to make my *shivah* call. I had been told that the house was crowded with people dropping in, besides the relatives from out-of-state. I was startled, nevertheless, to be greeted by the sound of music, raised voices, laughter, instead of the hushed sounds of a house of mourning. In the softly-carpeted living room, women were serving drinks, passing plates of refreshments, talking. Finally, I spied Yisroel's father, sitting on a low stool. Grey-faced and unshaven, he looked twenty years older than I remembered him. But he spoke to me cordially.

"Some *shivah*, Rabbi. More like a cocktail party. I keep telling them all to go home, but I guess they like my booze." He removed his glasses, rubbed his eyes slowly. "Listen, the kids are in the rec room over there, watching TV. Yisroel will be glad to see you."

Yisroel was not glad to see me. He was flustered and embarrassed. "Hey, Rabbi, what are you doing here? I mean, aren't you supposed to be in school? Oh, it's not three o'clock yet." Nervously, he offered me a drink of soda. He scanned the table, crowded with refreshments. "I guess there's nothing you can eat here." His face brightened suddenly. "I know. We've got some kosher potato chips somewhere, the kind we used for the school party." He stepped over the incumbent form of his brother, and standing in the doorway of the crowded living room, called, "Hey Mom, have we got . . . ."

There had been a lull in the conversation. Now there was a sudden frozen silence. The words hung in the air for a moment, then were mercifully covered by conversation. Yisroel's brother got up and left the room. I couldn't bring myself to look at Yisroel. To have lost your mother was bad enough. But to have been so dumb as to forget that she was dead, that she was not there, would never be there, to answer you when you called her . . . When I finally looked at him, he was slumped in his seat, staring blindly at the TV screen. The look of bewilderment in his gray eyes was more terrible than tears.

Little wonder that he was bewildered. I looked at the shelves of the rec room, crowded with every expensive gadget. Had Yisroel ever been refused or denied anything for long, in his young life? Had he ever been asked to renounce, to sacrifice, even a piece of gum because it wasn't kosher, or a ball game because it was Shabbat? How was he to understand, this child who had always had all that this rich land could offer, that he could not have the person he needed most in the world?

It was getting late. In fifteen minutes, I had to be in class. I rose, touched Yisroel's thin shoulders. "I've got to be going, Yisroel." He rose, politely, to walk me to the door. In the hallway, I murmured the traditional words, and translated, "May G-d comfort you, Yisroel." The boy looked at me with uncomprehending grey eyes, and I realized the words meant nothing to him. "G-d" was a word that belonged in Hebrew school. It had no reality in his life. As for turning to his Father in Heaven for comfort in his hour of great need, where would Yisroel have learned to do that? He had never seen his mother wipe away a tear as she lit the Shabbat candles. He had never seen his father crying quietly into his *tallit* on Yom Kippur. And I, his teacher, the only Rebbe that he had, who told him he must *daven* for fifteen minutes every day, had I done any better? No, I realized with sudden, bitter recognition. I prided myself on being a chassid, but I had taught with my head alone, had been afraid to open my heart to the children. Words that had not come from the heart, little wonder they did not enter the heart.

Yisroel stood patiently, waiting for me to go. Instead, I sat down on the built-in bench in the hallway. "Sit down for a minute, Yisroel."

The boy sat, warily, on the edge of his seat.

"Yisroel," I began, "are you saying Kaddish for your mother?"

He looked frightened. "Kaddish? Oh. They made us say something when we were standing by . . . when we were standing . . . "

"By the grave?" I prompted him gently.

The boy nodded, his eyes far away, seeing again what he had tried to forget.

"And now," I persisted. "In the mornings. Who says it when the men come here to *daven*?"

"I don't know," he said vaguely, dully. "My uncle, I guess. The one from Florida."

"Yisroel." I put my arm around him, and drew him close to me. His small body was stiff, clenched tight as a fist, but he did not pull away from me. "You should be saying Kaddish for your mother. You and your brothers."

"Why?"

I groped for words, trying to explain what Kaddish meant, to the child who said it, to the soul that had passed on to eternity, to the Jewish people. The boy's intent grey eyes were upon me. Suddenly, I had an idea.

"Yisroel, I'm going to tell you a story. It's about another boy, a Jewish boy whose name was also Yisroel."

I told him about the small boy, sleeping in a room with an earthen floor, in another time, another land. His mother, a poor widow, a maid in the houses of the rich, gently shakes him out of his sleep. Together they walk through the still-dark streets to the shul. The boy wears threadbare clothing, broken shoes; he has nothing. But he is rich in faith and courage. The memory of his father is always with him, and he knows that G-d, the Father of

Orphans is watching over him. The boy begins to recite the Kaddish in his child's voice. His mother, broken by poverty and grief, cries happy tears in the balcony. And thousands of angels, his father's holy soul among them, descend to hear Yisroel say Kaddish.

Later, the same boy, orphaned of his mother as well, walks alone and unafraid in the forest, for he fears no one and nothing, only G-d alone. There, undisturbed, he pours out his holy soul before the King of the world.

"And the boy," I concluded, "grew up to be the great Baal Shem Tov, whose name you bear."

Yisroel had listened silently to my story, all the time crushing and straightening a paper cup in his hands. At last, still without looking at me and in a voice so low I had to bend close to hear, he asked, "If I say it, say Kaddish, can she hear me?"

Minutes later, we sat, Yisroel and I, bent over a Siddur we had found in the bookshelf, like two conspirators. Yisroel repeated the words, until he was satisfied he could read them without a mistake. We agreed that he would say it with his uncle for the rest of the week. After that, he would come to shul, every day.

"Remember, Yisroel, if there is no one to take you, give me a call. I'll pick you up." I left him, looking after me through the glass door. I was more than half an hour late for Hebrew school.

I did not see Yisroel for the rest of the *shivah* week. But his bereavement had made him a sort of class hero, and I was kept posted on his activities. They had seen him at basketball in the center, he had come to David's birthday party. His father had been in the hospital for two days but was home now. On Sunday he would go skiing. He would not be back in school until next Tuesday.

"What a vacation," sighed one boy enviously. "Well, you would also want a vacation if your mother died."

"G-d forbid," I interjected, with a sigh. It was clear that kind friends and relatives were keeping the boy as busy as possible, to take his mind off his troubles. Saying Kaddish at six-thirty in the morning did not seem to fit

into this agenda. I had little hope of seeing him in the shabby downtown shul on the coming Tuesday.

But there, on that bleak and grey Tuesday morning, looking strangely out of place among the gnarled old men who made up the weekday *minyan,* stood Yisroel. Hands in his pocket, he was studying, with elaborate casualness, the brass name plaques on the wall.

His face lit up when he saw me. "Oh, there you are, Rabbi. I didn't think you were coming!"

"And I didn't think you were," I rejoined. We laughed.

"My father brought me. It was pitch black when we woke up. We didn't even have breakfast yet."

"It was crazy to wake him this early." Gently his father straightened Yisroel's kipah. "But what could I do. The kid wanted to come, not his brothers, just the little one."

Yisroel was beginning to squirm with embarrassment from all this attention, but at that moment the services began, he started to shake up and down like a cork, trying to keep up with the tempo of the grown-up davening. I also had trouble keeping up with the working-men's minyan, and didn't realize the time had come for Kaddish until I felt the boy's tight grip on my arm.

The lectern was too high, so Yisroel held the Siddur in his hands. A hush had fallen over the small group. Yisroel's high, clear voice trembled slightly, but he began bravely. *Yisgadal v'yiskadash shmei rabah.* At the end, the words were muffled by his tears, but by then he was not the only one who was crying.

"Not bad for a kid of eleven." The doctor blew his nose loudly. "I don't know if I ever told you this, Rabbi, but his great-grandfather was a famous Rabbi in Russia. A scholar."

We walked out into the bright daylight. It was going to be a fine winter's day after all.

"Rabbi," Yisroel spoke to me. His small, smudged face looked pale and peaked in the brilliant sun. His bangs straggled unkempt into his eyes. But those grey eyes looked straight at me, no longer lost and bewildered. "I'll come every day. I'll come for the whole year."

Yisroel's father was not doing well. He was in and out of the hospital all that winter. "It's no good, Rabbi." He thumped his chest angrily. "It's no good in there. What's going to be with my little one, my Yisroel?"

So, in the end, it was I who drove past Yisroel's house in my rattling Chevy, and picked him up on my way to shul. Driving through the quiet grey streets, as the dawn slowly illuminated the world, we talked. At first, casually, about school, sports, cars, Bar Mitzvah. Then came the questions, at first shyly, hesitantly, then in a rush. "Could a boy light Shabbat candles? Could you make a brachah on lobster? Kiddush on bagels? If G-d loves the Jews, why did we suffer so much? Could you jog to shul on Shabbat if it was too far to walk? If you couldn't handle money on Shabbat, could you tell the storekeeper to take it out of your pockets? Could you say the Shema a second time, if you woke up with nightmare? What if there was a good person, a really good man, but he didn't believe in the Torah?"

Some of the questions broke my heart. Others were funny, but I couldn't laugh. How can you laugh at a Jew's first, faltering steps toward Yiddishkeit?

Of his mother, he spoke to me only once.

—"Is Moshiach really going to come?"

—"He really is, and very soon."

—"Is it true what you said, that all the . . . dead people will come back to life?"

—"Would I lie to you, Yisroel?"

—"No, I don't think you lied to me. It's just that I miss her, I miss her so much."

Winter changed into delicate spring and a golden summer. People in Lowell found it hard to believe that Yisroel was still saying Kaddish.

The boys in school reminded each other, "Don't give Yisroel a Siddur. He davens with the men." "Still?" "Still."

"Plenty of people could learn from him," the *minyan-men* nodded at each other. They plied Yisroel with herring and crackers. It was with difficulty I restrained them from giving him a shot glass of *shnaps*.

"I don't understand it." His father shakes his head, puzzled. "He never kept up anything this long, not even Little League. And you know something," his lined, bitter face softened, as it always did when he spoke of his youngest son. "He lights the candles every Friday night. Then—he does this all by himself—he takes the small challahs you give him, he covers them, he makes Kiddush." He chuckled suddenly. "The other day the housekeeper is bringing him his supper, those little baby hams. He shakes his head, and says, 'I'm not eating this. It's not kosher.' So I say to him, 'Yisroel, it doesn't make sense. Everything in the house is *traif*, the sea food, the meat, our dishes.' And do you know what he said? He said, 'You've got to start somewhere!' A kid of eleven. 'You've got to start somewhere.'"

Mr. Gruber had begun to teach him his Bar Mitzvah lessons. "I've had his brothers for five years. Zero. Absolutely nothing. This kid wants to learn. I've finally got a student instead of a tape recorder. It's a miracle."

But I wasn't surprised. And I thought I knew when the miracle had happened. It was the day a frightened and grieving child listened to the story of the Baal Shem Tov, the tzaddik who knows how to reveal the spark that lies hidden deep in the soul of every Jew.

Originally published in *Di Yiddishe Heim Journal*
Reprinted with permission from www.chabad.org

Are We Disposable?

By Jay Litvin

Not long ago, I was in a meeting with someone whose husband had passed away less than a year before. In the midst of the meeting someone cracked a joke and the woman of whom I'm speaking laughed. I was startled. "How can you laugh?" I thought. "Your spouse passed away less than a year ago!" And then an alarming thought occurred to me: "Are we all disposable and that easily replaceable? Can our loved ones laugh so quickly after we're gone?"

Right now and before writing another word, I want to clear up any misconceptions: Within seconds of thinking this I knew that that's not what I really think. My wife suggested that perhaps my own condition had something to do with my response. Being in remission from lymphoma does not mean that I believe 100% of the time that I'm out of the woods. Mainly, I'm very optimistic. But I'm not Mr. Bitachon every second of every day. And, whenever I hear of someone who passes away from some version of what I have (or, please G-d, had), it reopens unpleasant thoughts and fears. Unfortunately, hearing about such people is all too common these days.

"It was laughter with a broken heart that will never mend in full," my wife assured me.

Are we disposable? Sounds ridiculous doesn't it? And of course we are not. But death is not the only place I find evidence to my fear that our lives are too quickly forgotten and replaced not only by laughter, but by others.

Look at divorce. People marry. People divorce. Their spouse remarries. And there is someone else who comes to take his or her place. In some cases, he or she comes to parent the children. Now you see him, now you don't. There seems to be this space—husband, father, whatever—that can be filled by a variety of candidates. Perhaps not in the same way, but still . . . filled. What is the message to our children? He was your Daddy. But he can be your Daddy, too.

I'm taking a risk here. I know that what I'm writing is an exaggeration, and certainly not the most rational or wisest train of thought. I'm inviting you on a journey with my darker side. My fearful side. The side that emerges when my worst nightmares and thoughts overpower my higher and better self. Can I trust you to come along without too much judgment? Will you hang in there with me a little while longer as I flush this out?

If Daddies are replaceable, is the same true of the children? In a disposable, replaceable world, do we need ponder too long why kids sometimes wonder if their lives are worth anything? Why we sometimes wonder the same?

But, when we lose someone in our life there is a dilemma. On the one hand we are to mourn. On the other, we are to carry on with our lives. And, in today's modern world, it seems that the faster and fuller we do this, the healthier we are. Rarely, today, do we see a widow or widower whose loss is worn constantly on his sleeve. Whose grief becomes an indelible look in the eyes and tension on the face. And even though someone may have once been the "love of my life," in today's world it seems that after loss we are encouraged to pick ourselves up and begin a new life. But if one creates a new life can't one also then have a new "love of my life"? New life; new love. Disposable life; replaceable love.

I'm traveling further downward. Spinning really. Can you feel it? I've done this before, but it's different having you with me. And not even knowing who you are: faceless, unknown confidants!

Have I come to the point where I trust you all so much? Or is it just the chemo and past months of battle that have left me not even caring what you think?

Perhaps if I thought about my own parents more. Perhaps if they occupied more of my thoughts and speech? Perhaps if I didn't feel that my own life had continued on so easily after they both passed away? Were they disposable? Of course not. Were they replaceable? Impossible. And yet . . .

No, I don't want anyone to suffer after loss. Not anyone in my family. Not anyone in yours. I want for there to be laughter again. Full lives. Happiness. Joy. Song. A warm, lively Shabbos table filled with children and grandchildren, great-grandchildren. Even the ones I might never meet.

But, oh, how I don't want ever to be forgotten. For life to be as if I never was. Can you understand that? Do you ever feel that? Someone told me recently that they never think about one day not being here, yet for me, not one day passes without that thought.

They say "Jacob lived through the good deeds of his children." But that was Jacob. And look at who his children were. But what about me?

Have you never thought these thoughts? Never felt the fear? Never been caught in the spiral of your own darker self with no escape in view? Never wished you could ascend towards the point of light you know is there, somewhere . . . but where?

I'm lucky enough to have a person in my life who motivates me to reach a little higher, and helps me get there some of the time. His name is Rav (Rabbi) Gluckowsky. He's the guy in my community who is my teacher and guide. He's someone I learn from not just in a class, but from the way he lives his life.

(A lot of people call him by his first name, but I prefer to always call him "Rav Gluckowsky," even though we're pretty good friends and I'm older by a long shot. Perhaps it's because we're friends that I call him "Rav." I enjoy giving things to my friends. And, in this case, I enjoy giving respect to someone I like very much. The respect and honor I afford him in no way lessens the familiarity and comfort I feel when I'm with him. He is my Rav and we are friends.)

I never met Rav Gluckowsky's father. And yet he accompanies Rav Gluckowsky almost everywhere he goes and certainly in most every meeting I have with him. There is not a talk Rav Gluckowsky gives in which he doesn't quote his father. The other day we were speaking of our sons' singing in the choir and he mentioned what a great voice his father had. Last week I went to a birthday farbrengen and Rav Gluckowsky was asked to tell a story. "Let me tell you a story about the previous Rebbe that my father used to tell . . ." He not only told the story in his father's name, his father was imbedded throughout the story.

His father's picture hangs prominently in his living room. We are invited to his home several times a year to share in some event commemorating his father. And one has the feeling that Rav Gluckowsky's entire life is dedicated to his father, that he is busily and consciously being the son his father would have wanted him to be.

In shul, we all know that many of the tunes he sings during davening come from his father. And in our community, we all know we are the beneficiaries of the wonderful man Rav Gluckowsky's father must have been. We, too, are better off because Rav Gluckowsky's father's presence once blessed the earth.

Would Sukkot be Sukkot without the stories of the sukkahs that Rav Gluckowsky built together with his father and brothers? How many times have we heard the one about the last minute car ride with the police chasing behind just minutes before candle lighting time? Would our boys' school be the same if it was not filled with the educational adages from Rav Gluckowsky's father, an educator who taught first through eighth grades in Toronto for forty years?

And would we not all love to say to our children as Rav Gluckowsky recently said to his: How proud I would be if you grew up to be a teacher like Zaidy, a man who, through his teaching, improved the lives of so many, many people.

Funny, but when I finally saw a video of Rav Gluckowsky's father, he looked like an ordinary guy. A school teacher. Someone a lot like you and I. But someone who had risen to near mythic stature through the love, respect and devotion of his son.

Listening to Rav Gluckowsky, I, this ordinary father, could imagine one day being lifted to such heights by my own children. And such fantasies fill me with warmth and courage. They ease my fears. They impel me forward to live a life full of actions that will give my children something to talk about one day to their children and to their communities.

If Rav Gluckowsky's father is not disposable, neither am I. Neither are you. We are as irreplaceable as the love we give. Our indelible mark is invisibly carved on the hearts of our children and loved ones. Our mark is contained not only in their laughter, but in the laughter they impart to others. Laughter, as my wife says, that comes from a broken heart.

But a heart filled with love breaks and then grows stronger through mending. Its strength comes from its softness, a softness made softer by the love we left behind, perhaps softer, even, through the loss our children feel after we've left.

The woman who laughed came into my office the other day. She stopped by to tell me about the event held in her community the night before to commemorate the first anniversary of her husband's passing. She described the event for a long time and then went on to tell me about the highlight of the evening.

"My daughter read a letter she had written to her Abba," she began. "In the letter she described all the family events of the past year. She described them in detail so that my husband, her father, would be able to take nachas from her piano recital, from her brother's first bike ride, from the first day mommy was able to go back to work after months of feeling too sad to even leave the house . . . "

As the woman spoke her eyes welled with tears. They never spilled over. It was as if her heart had simply filled with so much love it had to relieve itself through her eyes.

She stood in my doorway for a long time reciting all the events that her daughter had recounted in her letter to her father. She even told me how her daughter had described to her father what she knew her father's reactions would be. "You would have laughed so hard, Abba . . . " "You would have told us your famous story about the time you . . . " "Oh, Abba, how you would have enjoyed the music . . . "

I never grew tired of listening to this woman tell about this evening of remembrance. Long past the time when I should have returned to my work, I listened attentively about her children and their love for their father and for his memory.

And when she finally finished and continued down the hall, I could have continued listening even longer.

But instead I sat down and wrote this article. Perhaps one day my children will read it. Or, better yet, perhaps they'll read to their children one day.

May I live to be 120.

Editor's note: Jay sent chabad.org this article at a time when—as he writes in its opening paragraphs—he was very optimistic about his prognosis. But shortly thereafter, while still working on the article, a blood test result brought the news that his illness had turned once more aggressive. Indeed, such ups-and-downs often occurred during his valiant four-year battle with the disease.

Because of the unfortunate turn of events, Jay felt that the subject of this article was too "close to home" to publish. Now, after the worst has occurred, Jay's family decided that the time has come to share it with our readers.

Reprinted with permission from www.chabad.org

Lesson **6**
The Ultimate Moment

Introduction

We have come to the end of our *Soul Quest.* We have spoken of the creation of souls, birth, life, death, Paradise, reincarnation, and the relationship with past lives. But what is the ultimate destination of our journey? In this lesson, you will discover the surprising answer.

Power of the Day

Learning Activity 1

What is the most important day on the Jewish calendar?

Be prepared to justify your answer.

Rabbi Chaim ibn Atar (1696–1743). Famed Talmudist, biblical exegete and kabbalist; author of *Or HaChaim*, a popular commentary on the Torah. Born in Meknes, Morocco, he was a prominent member of the Moroccan rabbinate. En route to Israel, he helped establish a yeshivah in Livorno, Italy. Arriving in Jerusalem in 1742, he remained active in the local *yeshivot*. The famed Jewish historian and bibliophile, Rabbi Chaim Joseph David Azulai, is among his most notable disciples.

Text 1

Each soul is split up into many sparks, and a number of these sparks are assigned to particular incarnations of the general soul. According to the number of sparks [of this particular incarnation], so is the number of the days of its life. On each day that [the person] fulfills the mitzvot, one spark of [the incarnation] is repaired, corresponding to this particular day.

RABBI CHAIM IBN ATAR, OR HACHAIM, BEREISHIT/GENESIS 47:29

Text 2 📜

אדם דואג על איבוד דמיו ואינו דואג על איבוד ימיו

דמיו אינם עוזרים ימיו אינם חוזרים

ספר החיים בשם "אמרי אנשי"

People worry about the loss of a dime, and not about the loss of their time. Their money will cut them no slack, and their days will never come back.

JEWISH PROVERB, CITED IN RABBI SHIMON HADARSHAN OF FRANKFURT, SEFER HACHAIM

Text 3 📜

Time must be guarded . . . . Every bit of time, every day that passes, is not just a day but an entire life's theme.

RABBI MENACHEM MENDEL SCHNEERSON, HAYOM YOM, CHESHVAN 17

Rabbi Menachem Mendel Schneerson (1902–1994). Known as "the Lubavitcher Rebbe," or simply as "the Rebbe." Born in southern Ukraine. Rabbi Schneerson escaped from the Nazis, arriving in the US in June 1941. The towering Jewish leader of the twentieth century, the Rebbe inspired and guided the revival of traditional Judaism after the European devastation, and often emphasized that the performance of just one additional good deed could usher in the era of Mashiach.

Text 4 📜

ושלא יניח שום יום מעשיית מצוה

צוואת הריב"ש א

Do not allow a single day to pass without performing a mitzvah.

RABBI YISRAEL BAAL SHEM TOV, TZAVA'AT HARIVASH, CHAPTER 1

Rabbi Yisrael ben Eliezer (1698–1760). Better known as the Baal Shem Tov or by the acronym Besht; rabbi and mystic; founder of the chassidic movement. Born in Okupy, Ukraine, he was orphaned as a child. The Baal Shem Tov served as a teacher and clay-digger, before founding the chassidic movement. Although he never committed his ideas to writing, the Baal Shem Tov's teachings were gathered by his disciples in various volumes.

Obstacle Course

Text 5

והנה מודעת זאת מארז״ל שתכלית בריאת עולם הזה הוא שנתאוה
הקב״ה להיות לו דירה בתחתונים (תנחומא נשא טז). . . . והנה תכלית
השתלשלו׳ העולמו׳ וירידתם ממדרגה למדרגה אינו בשביל עולמות
העליוני׳ . . . אלא התכלית הוא עו״הז התחתון שכך עלה ברצונו ית׳ להיות
נחת רוח לפניו ית׳ כד אתכפיא ס״א ואתהפך חשוכא לנהורא שיאיר אור
ה׳ אין סוף ב״ה במקום החשך והס״א של כל עוה״ז כולו ביתר שאת ויתר
עז ויתרון אור מן החשך מהארתו בעולמות עליונים

תניא פרק לו

"The purpose for which this world was created is that G-d desired to have an abode in the lowest realm (Midrash Tanchuma, *Naso* 16)." The purpose of the evolution [*hishtalshelut*] of the worlds and of their descent from level to level, is not for the sake of the higher worlds . . . . Rather, the purpose of this evolution is this lowest world.

For such was His will—that He find it pleasurable when the negative is subjugated [to holiness], and the darkness is transformed into [holy] light. This is in order that in the place of the darkness and negative that prevail throughout this world, the *Ein Sof* [light of G-d] will shine forth with greater strength and intensity—and with the superior quality of light that emerges from the darkness—than its radiance in the higher worlds.

RABBI SHNE'UR ZALMAN OF LIADI, TANYA, CHAPTER 36

Rabbi Shne'ur Zalman of Liadi (1745–1812). Known as "the Alter Rebbe" and "the Rav"; Born in Liozna, Belarus; buried in Hadiach, Ukraine; chassidic Rebbe and founder of the Chabad movement; among the principal students of the Magid of Mezeritch. His numerous works include the *Tanya,* an early classic of Chassidism; *Torah Or* and *Likutei Torah*; and *Shulchan Aruch HaRav,* a rewritten code of Jewish law. He was succeeded by his son, Rabbi Dovber of Lubavitch.

"A person's steps are established by G-d (Tehilim/Psalms 37:23)." This means that this particular soul must purify and improve something specific in a particular place. For centuries, or even since the world's creation, that which needs purification or improvement waits for this soul to come and purify or improve it. The soul too, has been waiting, ever since it came into being, for its time to descend, so that it can discharge the tasks of purification and improvement assigned to it.

HAYOM YOM, OP. CIT., ELUL 3

The Cycle of the Day
Night Shift

Text 7 ▐

שינה אחד מששים למיתה

תלמוד בבלי ברכות נז,ב

Sleep is one-sixtieth of death.

TALMUD, BERACHOT 57B

Text 8 ▐

דהא לית לך בר נש בעלמא דלא טעים טעמא דמותא בליליא ורוח מסאבא
שריא על ההוא גופא מאי טעמא בגין דנשמתא קדישא אסתלקת מניה דבר
נש ונפקת מניה, ועל דנשמתא קדישא נפקת ואסתלקת מניה שריא רוחא
מסאבא על ההוא גופא ואסתאב וכד נשמתא אתהדרת לגופא אתעבר ההוא
זוהמא והא אתמר דידוי דבר נש זוהמא דמסאבו אשתאר בהו

זוהר א קפד,ב

Rabbi Shimon bar Yochai (2nd century CE). Known by the acronym Rashbi; scholar of the Mishnah and founder of Jewish mysticism; an eminent disciple of Rabbi Akiva. The kabbalistic classic *Sefer HaZohar* is attributed to him and his disciples. Because of the Roman persecutions he was forced to hide with his son Eliezer for 13 years. Lag Ba'Omer is commemorated as the day of his passing, with thousands visiting his grave in Meron, Israel.

Every person has a foretaste of death during the night, because the holy soul then leaves, and the unclean spirit rests on the body and makes it unclean. When, however, the soul returns to the body, the pollution disappears, save from the person's hands, which retain it and thus remain unclean.

RABBI SHIMON BAR YOCHAI, ZOHAR I, 184B

Text 9

Why did G-d create people in a manner in which they are required to sleep? For humans were created to serve their master through the study of Torah and the fulfillment of mitzvot. Why then are people required to interrupt their service and devote several hours each day to sleep?

This question can be resolved as follows: The purpose for the creation of humans is to elevate the entire creation and bring it to a higher level of completion . . . . G-d created the world in a manner which leaves room for people to become "partners in creation," and reveal a new dimension in existence . . . .

Similarly, within each person's individual service, once a person has become accustomed to a specific pattern of behavior, it is necessary to strive to reach a new and higher peak . . . . This new dimension of service is reflected in the fact that each day, one's activity is interrupted through sleeping, and one awakens the next morning as a "new creation." Were a person to continue the study of Torah and fulfillment of mitzvot without interruption, this aspect of newness would not be revealed. Since one's service would be constant, any increase would follow as a natural and gradual progression, rather than as a radical change.

By contrast, when people are created in a manner in which they are required to sleep and thus interrupt their service, G-d emphasizes the importance of newness and how man has the potential to introduce this element into his service of G-d. Furthermore, since this dimension of newness requires an interruption, this interruption can be seen as part of the service of G-d infused by the quality of newness.

Thus . . . there is a descent for the sake of an ascent. Were a person to continue his service in a constant pattern of growth, the new dimension of ascent could not be perceived. By contrast, when there is an interruption in the pattern of growth, one is able to perceive the new quality in the ascent. Furthermore, the dimension of newness in an ascent which follows a descent allows for an ascent of a greater degree.

RABBI MENACHEM MENDEL SCHNEERSON,
TORAT MENACHEM 5750, VOLUME 4

Text 10

The reciting of *Shema* before retiring at night is, in miniature form, like the confession before death.

HAYOM YOM, OP. CIT., KISLEV 6

Text 11 📜

רבונו של עולם הריני מוחל לכל מי שהכעיס והקניט אותי או שחטא כנגדי
בין בגופי בין בממוני בין בכבודי בין בכל אשר לי
בין באונס בין ברצון בין בשוגג בין במזיד בין בדיבור בין במעשה
בין בגלגול זה בין בגלגול אחר לכל בר ישראל ולא יענש שום אדם בסיבתי
יהי רצון מלפניך ה׳ אלקי ואלקי אבותי שלא אחטא עוד
ולא אחזור בהם ולא אשוב עוד להכעיסך ולא אעשה הרע בעיניך
ומה שחטאתי מחוק ברחמיך הרבים ולא על ידי יסורים וחולאים רעים
יהיו לרצון אמרי פי והגיון לבי לפניך ה׳ צורי וגואלי

סידור נוסח האריז״ל, קריאת שמע על המטה

Master of the universe! I hereby forgive anyone who has angered or vexed me, or sinned against me, either physically or financially, against my honor or anything else that is mine, whether accidentally or intentionally, inadvertently or deliberately, by speech or by deed, in this incarnation or in any other—any Israelite; may no one be punished on my account.

May it be Your will, Lord my God and God of my fathers, that I shall sin no more nor repeat my sins, neither shall I again anger You nor do what is wrong in Your eyes. The sins I have committed, erase in Your abounding mercies, but not through suffering or severe illnesses. May the words of my mouth and the meditation of my heart be acceptable before You, Lord, my Strength and my Redeemer.

Siddur, Nusach HaAriZal, Prayer Before Retiring at Night

Text 12 📖

דבכל ליליא ולילא עד לא ישכב ועד לא נאים בעי בר נש למעבד חושבנא
מעובדוי דעבד כל ההוא יומא ויתוב מנייהו ויבעי עלייהו רחמי מאי טעמא
בההיא שעתא בגין דהההיא שעתא אילנא דמותא שארי בעלמא וכל בני
עלמא טעמין טעמא דמותא ובעי בההיא שעתא
למעבד חושבנא מעובדוי ויודי עלייהו

זוהר ג קעח,א

Each and every night before one goes to sleep, one must make an accounting of all of his deeds that he did that day. He should repent and ask for mercy. At that time, the tree of death resides in the world and all taste the taste of death. Therefore, one needs to make an accounting of his deeds and confess them.

ZOHAR, OP. CIT., III, 178A

Text 13a 📖

בְּיָדְךָ אַפְקִיד רוּחִי פָּדִיתָה אוֹתִי ה׳ אֵ-ל אֱמֶת

תהלים לא,ו

I entrust my spirit into Your hand; You will redeem me, L-rd, G-d of truth.

PSALMS 31:6

Text 13b 📖

הנשמה הזו ממלאה את כל הגוף

ובשעה שאדם ישן היא עולה ושואבת לו חיים מלמעלה

בראשית רבה יד,ט

The *neshamah* (soul) fills the body, and when the person sleeps, the soul ascends and draws life from above.

BEREISHIT RABAH 14:9

Dawning of the Day

Text 13c 📖

בשר ודם מפקידין בידו חדשים, ושוהין אצלו, והוא מחזירן בלויים וישנים

אבל הקב"ה מפקידין בידו בליין ושחוקין, והוא מחזירן חדשים

מדרש תהלים כה,ב

When one deposits a new item with a person, he returns it worn and old. But with regard to G-d, we deposit our soul worn and torn, and He returns it to us new.

MIDRASH TEHILIM 25:2

Text 14

מוֹדֶה אֲנִי לְפָנֶיךָ

מֶלֶךְ חַי וְקַיָּם שֶׁהֶחֱזַרְתָּ בִּי נִשְׁמָתִי בְּחֶמְלָה

רַבָּה אֱמוּנָתֶךָ

סידור נוסח האריז״ל, ברכות השחר

offer thanks to You, living and eternal King, for having restored my soul within me with mercy. Your faithfulness is great.

SIDDUR, NUSACH HAARIZAL, OP. CIT., PRAYER UPON ARISING

מוֹדֶה אֲנִי לְפָנֶיךָ

Learning Activity 2 *Modeh Ani* Contemplation Table 6.1 Worksheet

מוֹדֶה	*Modeh*	[I] Thank
אֲנִי	*Ani*	I
לְפָנֶיךָ	*Lefanecha*	Before You
מֶלֶךְ	*Melech*	King
חַי	*Chai*	Living

וְקַיָּם	**Vekayam**	**And existing**
שֶׁהֶחֱזַרְתָּ	**Shehechezarta**	**For You have returned**
בִּי נִשְׁמָתִי	**Bi Nishmati**	**My soul within me**
בְּחֶמְלָה	**Bechemlah**	**With Mercy.**
רַבָּה אֱמוּנָתֶךָ	**Rabah Emunatecha**	**Great is Your trustworthiness.**

Arriving at Your Final Destination

Text 15 📜

אל יאמר אדם הריני עושה מצות התורה ועוסק בחכמתה כדי שאקבל
כל הברכות הכתובות בה או כדי שאזכה לחיי העולם הבא, ואפרוש מן
העבירות שהזהירה תורה מהן כדי שאנצל מן הקללות הכתובות בתורה או
כדי שלא אכרת מחיי העולם הבא, אין ראוי לעבוד את ה׳ על הדרך הזה,
שהעובד על דרך זה הוא עובד מיראה. . . .

העובד מאהבה עוסק בתורה ובמצות והולך בנתיבות החכמה לא מפני דבר
בעולם ולא מפני יראת הרעה ולא כדי לירש הטובה אלא עושה האמת מפני
שהוא אמת וסוף הטובה לבא בגללה

משנה תורה הלכות תשובה י,א-ב

A person should not say, "Behold, I am performing mitzvot and engaged in the study of the Torah so that I will receive all the blessing written therein, or in order to merit the world to come, and will refrain from all the prohibitions in the Torah in order to be saved from all the curses written therein, or so that I will not be cut off from the world to come." It is not fitting to serve G-d in this way. One who serves G-d in this way serves on the basis of fear . . . .

One who serves from love engages in Torah and mitzvot and walks in the paths of wisdom, without concern for any earthly matter; not because of fear of evil, not in order to inherit good [Paradise], but to engage in the

Rabbi Moshe ben Maimon (1135–1204). Better known as Maimonides or by the acronym Rambam. Born in Córdoba, Spain. After the conquest of Córdoba by the Almohads, who sought to forcibly convert the Jews to Islam, he fled and eventually settled in Cairo. There he became the leader of the Jewish community and served as court physician to the vizier of Egypt. His rulings on Jewish law are considered integral to the formation of halachic consensus. He is most noted for authoring the *Mishneh Torah*, an encyclopedic arrangement of Jewish law. His philosophical work, *Guide for the Perplexed*, is also well-known.

truth because it is true, and in the end, the good will naturally flow as a result . . . .

Rambam (Maimonides), Mishneh Torah, Laws of Repentance, 10:1-2

Text 16

The concept of the resurrection is well-known among all Jews, and there are none who dispute it.

This is its significance: The body and soul will be reunited once again after they have been separated [by death]. There is no Jew who disputes this, and it cannot be interpreted other than literally. One may not accept the view of any Jew who believes otherwise.

Rambam, Discourse on the Resurrection, Chapter 4

Text 17

ואני נבראתי לשמש את קוני

משנה קידושין ד,יד

I was created to serve my Maker.

Mishnah, Kidushin 4:14

Key Points

1. The most important day in the Jewish calendar is *today*.

2. Every moment is unique, invaluable, and irreplaceable.

3. The essence of life is growth and transformation, which necessitates constant challenges. View these challenges as opportunities for learning and growth.

4. Everything that occurs to us in life is assigned to us as part of our Divine mission.

5. Every day is a spiritual birth and death—waking and sleep.

6. Prepare for sleep by refocusing on our mission, confession, and forgiveness.

7. Begin each day with a moment of mindfulness and gratitude, remembering our mission.

8. Center your life on the here and now—this is our ultimate destination.

Additional Readings

The Meaning of Death

By **Rabbi Maurice Lamm**

What is death? Is it merely the cessation of the biological function of living? Is it but the tragedy to end all other tragedies? Is it simply the disappearance of the soul, the end of consciousness, the evaporation of personality, the disintegration of the body into its elemental components? Is it an end beyond which there is only black void? Or, is there a significance, some deep and abiding meaning to death—one that transcends our puny ability to understand?

With all of modern man's sophistication, his brilliant technological achievements, the immense progress of his science, his discovery of new worlds of thought, he has not come one iota closer to grasping the meaning of death than did his ancient ancestors. Philosophers and poets have probed the idea of immortality, but stubbornly it remains, as always, the greatest paradox of life.

In practice, however, we must realize that what death means to the individual depends very much on what life means to him.

If life is a stage, and we the poor players who strut and fret our hour upon the stage and then are heard no more; if life is a tale told by an idiot, full of sound and fury, signifying nothing; if life is an inconsequential drama, a purposeless amusement—then death is only the heavy curtain that falls on the final act. It sounds its hollow thud: *É Finita la commedia,* and we are no more. Death has no significance, because life itself has no lasting meaning.

If life is only the arithmetic of coincidence, man a chance composite of molecules, the world an haphazard conglomeration without design or purpose, where everything is temporal and nothing eternal—with values dictated only by consensus—then death is merely the check-mate to an interesting, thoughtful, but useless game of chance. Death has no transcendent significance, since nothing in life has had transcendent significance. If such is the philosophy of life, death is meaningless, and the deceased need merely be disposed of unceremoniously, and as efficiently as possible.

If life is only nature mindlessly and compulsively spinning its complicated web, and man only a high-level beast, and the world—in Schopenhauer's phrase—*eine grosse schlachtfeld*, a great battlefield, and if values are only those of the jungle, aimed only at the satisfaction of animal appetites—then death is simply a further reduction to the basic elements, progress an adventure into nothingness, and our existence on this earth only a cosmic trap. In this scheme, life is surrounded by parentheses, dropped or substituted without loss of meaning to nature. Death, in this sense, is the end of a cruel match that pits man against beast, and man against man. It is the last slaughter. Furtively, irrevocably, despairingly, man sinks into the soil of a cold and impersonal nature, his life without purpose, his death without significance. His grave need not be marked. As his days were as a passing shadow, without substance and shape, so his final repose.

If life is altogether absurd, with man bound and chained by impersonal fate or ironbound circumstances, where he is never able to achieve real freedom and only dread and anguish prevail—then death is the welcome release from the chains of despair. The puppet is returned to the box, the string is severed, the strain is no more.

But if life is the creation of a benevolent God, the infusion of the Divine breath; if man is not only higher than the animal, but also "a little lower than the angels"; if he has a soul, as well as a body; if his relationship is not only the "I-it" of man and nature, but the "I-Thou" of creature with Creator; and if he tempers his passions with the moral commands of an eternal, transcendent God—then death is a return to the Creator at the time of death set by the Creator, and life-after-death the only way of a just and merciful and ethical God. If life has any significance, if it is not mere happenstance, then man knows that some day his body will be replaced, even as his soul unites with eternal God.

In immortality man finds fulfillment of all his dreams. In this religious framework, the sages equated this world with an anteroom to a great palace, the glorious realm of the future. For a truly religious personality, death has profound meaning, because for him life is a tale told by a saint. It is, indeed, full of sound and fury which sometimes signifies nothing, but often bears eloquent testimony to the Divine power that created and sustained him.

The rabbis say *hai alma k'bei hilula damya*, this world can be compared to a wedding. At a wedding two souls are united. In that relationship they bear the seed of the future. Ultimately, the partners to the wedding die— but the seed of life grows on, and death is conquered, for the seed of the future carries the germ of the past. This world is like unto a wedding.

Death has meaning if life had meaning. If one is not able to live, will he be able to die?

This is an excerpt from *The Jewish Way in Death and Mourning*, by Rabbi Maurice Lamm.

Reprinted with permission from www.chabad.org

Why Do We Sleep?

By **Yanki Tauber**

Every day, many billions of man-hours are slept down the drain. If there are 6,000,000,000 human beings in the world, and each sleeps an average of 7.2 hours a night— well, you do the math. The bottom line is that slumbered time is probably our most wasted human resource.

Why do we spend 25% to 30% of our lives doing nothing? Why do we sleep?

Perhaps this seems a pointless question. Why sleep? Because our body demands it of us.

Because that is how we are physiologically constructed— that we require so many hours of rest each day in order to function. But to the Jew, there are no pointless questions. If G-dcreated us a certain way, there is a reason. If our active hours must always be preceded by what the Talmud calls the "minor death" of sleep, there is a lesson here, a truth that is fundamental to the nature of human achievement.

The Lubavitcher Rebbe explains: If we didn't sleep, there would be no tomorrow. Life would be a single, seamless today. Our every thought and deed would be an outgrowth of all our previous thoughts and deeds. There would be no new beginnings in our lives, for the very concept of a new beginning would be alien to us.

Sleep means that we have the capacity to not only improve but also transcend ourselves. To open a new chapter in life that is neither predicted nor enabled by what we did and were up until now. To free ourselves of yesterday's constraints and build a new, recreated self.

Rabbi Israel Baal Shem Tov taught that G-dcreates the world anew every millisecond of time. If we are His "partners in creation" (as the Talmud says we are), we should be able to do that too—at least once a day.

Wake up tomorrow—and start anew.

Reprinted with permission from www.chabad.org

Acknowledgments

ife cycle events are often the impetus for exploration of the meaning and purpose of life. In the wake of a death, many people are prompted to study and reflection. It is not surprising then, that in the ten years since the **Rohr Jewish Learning Institute**'s launch, we have received numerous requests for a course dealing with life's biggest enigmas: birth, death, and the afterlife. The creation of a course that would adequately address this subject has been a vast collaborative effort.

The author of *Soul Quest*, **Rabbi Yisrael Rice**, is the chairman of the editorial board of the **JLI**, as well as a contributing author. He has long championed the idea of the looking at life's transitions from the perspective of the soul. A topic as central and vast as this elicits strong opinions about the best approach. Rabbi Rice has managed to graciously incorporate many suggestions while ensuring that the course remained faithful to his powerful vision. A thoughtful and empathic author, Rabbi Rice has also been an exceptional team leader for this project. May HaShem grant him success in all of his endeavors.

The **JLI** Editorial Board has provided invaluable assistance that has guided the development of the course. **Rabbi Yossi Nemes** provided extensive comments on the lesson drafts and offered creative suggestions for enhancing the inspirational content of the course. **Rabbi Avraham Sternberg** supplied valuable primary sources to enhance the depth of the lessons, and provided particular assistance with the development of Lesson Six. **Rabbi Yehuda Weg** and **Rabbi Benny Rapoport** made many useful comments on Lessons One and Two. **Mr. Yaakov Ort** served as editorial consultant and master brainstormer in the embryonic stages of the course, helping to identify the critical questions that a course like this must answer, and ensuring the relevance of the content to the average student. **Rabbi Sholom Raichik** and **Rabbi Shraga Sherman** piloted the course and gave many practical suggestions for revision. In particular, we thank Rabbi Raichik for comments on Lessons One, Four, and Six and Rabbi Sherman for comments on Lessons Two, Four, and Six.

We have been privileged to have the generous assistance of **Rabbi Yossi Paltiel** who brilliantly synthesized much of the scholarly thinking on the subject matter and provided notes and sources to enhance the teacher's manual. Rabbi Paltiel also prepared a summary of background material for the instructors, which he articulately presented at the **JLI** Instructors' Conference.

Rabbi Mordechai Dinerman, our dedicated research associate, approaches his work with careful precision and thoughtful analysis. He has an uncanny knack for discovering relevant and intriguing sources. Rabbi Dinerman contributed stories and texts, and graciously proofread the Hebrew in the textbook.

Rabbi Binyomin Walters provided the front and back matter for each chapter, and developed a number of new features to aid the instructor, most notably the lesson maps.

The **Rohr Jewish Learning Institute** is blessed with an exceptional production team. We thank **Mrs. Chana Lightstone** for her generous assistance with editorial production. Our thanks also to **Mrs. Ya'akovah Weber**, our dedicated and meticulous copyeditor; **Nachman Levine**, our layout designer and research editor, who brings to our work not only an artistic eye but a scholarly one; and **Mr. Shimon Leib Jacobs**, who prints and distributes our books with grace and efficiency.

Rabbi Mendy Halberstam, our outgoing marketing coordinator, has taught us much over the years about how to capture the essence of a course in a way that is both personal and engaging. His meticulous oversight of our campaigns has ensured that our message is always effectively promulgated in timely fashion. We wish him success in all his future endeavors. Our incoming marketing director, **Rabbi Saadya Notik**, brings verve, creativity, and freshness to his work. We warmly welcome him on board. Special thanks to **Rabbi Shraga Sherman**, who reviews our marketing materials, and our thanks, as well, to the members of our marketing board.

We thank **Spotlight Design** for the design of our textbook cover and **JLI** Multiplex pages.

Special thanks to **Chabad.org**, an invaluable online resource of Jewish learning and information, for providing many of the articles for our Additional Readings. Thanks also to **Rabbi Simon Jacobson** and **meaningfullife.com** for articles and video footage that have enhanced this course.

We thank **Mrs. Rivka Sternberg**, administrator of our flagship courses, for her conscientious attention to the smooth coordination of our process, from the inception stage to coordination. Her judgment and reliability are the pillars upon which our department stands. We wish her well as she embarks on a new move.

The hard work of our support staff at **JLI Central** is critical to the success of every project. **Rabbi Mendel Sirota** provides prompt and courteous customer support, for which **JLI** is famous, with warmth and efficiency. Mendel also handles our shipping and printing. **Rabbi Benny Rapoport** designs the PowerPoint presentations which enhance the teaching of every lesson, both visually and conceptually. **Mrs. Chana Lightstone** and **Rabbi Shmuel Klatzkin** provide editorial review for the PowerPoints. The weekly videos are produced under the talented and creative hand of **Rabbi Levi Teldon**. **Rabbi Mendel Bell** is in charge of our online division and ensures the integrity of our online environment. **Rabbi Levi Kaplan**'s keen assessment and practical approach have been helpful on many occasions. Our devoted affiliate liaisons, **Mrs. Mindy Wallach** and **Mrs. Musie Kesselman**, coordinate the many details that hone our professional edge to perfection. **Mrs. Shaina Basha Mintz** and **Mrs. Nechama Shmotkin** conscientiously oversee our accounts. **Rabbi Yoni Katz** coordinates our yearly Instructor's Conference.

We are immensely grateful for the encouragement of **JLI**'s chairman, and vice chairman of *Merkos L'Inyonei Chinuch*—Lubavitch World Headquarters, **Rabbi Moshe Kotlarsky**, as well as for the unwavering support of **JLI**'s principal patrons, **Mr. and Mrs. George and Pamela Rohr**. They have spearheaded the monumental growth of the organization from its inception to this very day.

The constant progress of **JLI** is a testament to the visionary leadership of our director, **Rabbi Efraim Mintz**, who is never content to rest on his laurels, and who boldly encourages continued innovation and change.

JLI's devoted executive board, **Rabbi Chaim Block**, **Rabbi Hesh Epstein**, **Rabbi Yosef Gansburg**, **Rabbi Shmuel Kaplan**, **Rabbi Avremel Sternberg**, and **Rabbi Yisrael Rice**, devote countless hours to the development of **JLI**. Their dedicated commitment and sage direction have helped **JLI** continue to grow and flourish.

Finally, **JLI** represents an incredible partnership of over 300 *shluchim* giving of their time and talent to further Jewish education. We thank them for generously sharing their thoughts, feedback, questions, and teaching experiences. They are our most valuable critics, and our most helpful contributors.

I am filled with gratitude to HaShem for having allowed me the privilege of being a part of this sacred work, inspired by the call of the Lubavitcher Rebbe, of righteous memory, to bring Torah to Jews all over the world, wherever they may be. I am humbled by the opportunity to partner with our affiliates all over the world in this vital mission, and pray that I do justice to the responsibility with which I am charged.

Chana Silberstein Ph.D.
Course Editor
Ithaca, New York
Elul 18, 5769

The Rohr Jewish Learning Institute

An affiliate of
Merkos L'Inyonei Chinuch
The Educational Arm of
The Chabad Lubavitch Movement
822 Eastern Parkway, Brooklyn, NY 11213

JLI Supplementary Courses

Rabbi Levi Kaplan
Director
Brooklyn, NY

Authors

Mrs. Chani Abehsera
Los Angeles, CA

Rabbi Zalman Abraham
Brooklyn, NY

Rabbi Levi Jacobson
Toronto, ON

Mrs. Malka Touger
Jerusalem, Israel

Mrs. Shimonah Tzukernik
Brooklyn, NY

JLI Teacher Training

Rabbi Berel Bell
Director
Montreal, QC

myShiur:
Advanced Learning Initiative

Rabbi Shmuel Kaplan
Chairman
Potomac, MD

Rabbi Levi Kaplan
Director

National Jewish Retreat

Rabbi Hesh Epstein
Chairman
Columbia, SC

Rabbi Yoni Katz
Director

Bruce Backman
Coordinator

Rabbi Avrumy Epstein
Liaison

Sinai Scholars Society
in partnership with
Chabad on Campus

Rabbi Menachem Schmidt
Chairman
Philadelphia, PA

Rabbi Moshe Chaim Dubrowski
Chabad on Campus

Rabbi Yitzchok Dubov
Director

Rabbi Lev Cotlar
Affiliate Liaison

Torah Café Online Learning

Rabbi Levi Kaplan
Director

Rabbi Simcha Backman
Consultant

Rabbi Mendel Bell
Webmaster

Getzy Raskin
Filming and Editing

Rabbi Mendy Elishevitz
Website Design

Moshe Raskin
Video Editing

Torah Studies

Rabbi Yossi Gansburg
Chairman
Toronto, ON

Rabbi Meir Hecht
Director

Rabbi Yechezkel Deitsch
Mrs. Nechama Shmotkin
Administrators

JLI Academy

Rabbi Hesh Epstein
Chairman

Rabbi Shmuel Wolvovsky
Director

Beis Medrosh L'Shluchim
in partnership with
Shluchim Exchange

Steering Committee

Rabbi Simcha Backman
Rabbi Mendy Kotlarsky
Rabbi Efraim Mintz

Rabbi Sholom Zirkind
Administrator

Rabbi Yitzchok Steiner
Coordinator

Rabbi Mendel Margolin
Producer

Advisory Board

Rabbi Yisroel Altein
Pittsburgh, PA

Rabbi Mendel Cohen
Sacramento, CA

Rabbi Mordechai Farkash
Bellevue, WA

Rabbi Mendel Lipsker
Sherman Oaks, CA

JLI Central
Founding Department Heads

Rabbi Zalman Charytan
Acworth, GA

Rabbi Mendel Druk
Cancun, Mexico

Rabbi Menachem Gansburg
Toronto, ON

Rabbi Chaim Zalman Levy
New Rochelle, NY

Rabbi Elchonon Tenenbaum
Napa Valley, CA

Rohr JLI Affiliates

Share the **Rohr JLI** experience with friends and relatives worldwide

ALABAMA
BIRMINGHAM
Rabbi Yossi Friedman
205.970.0100

ARIZONA
CHANDLER
Rabbi Mendel Deitsch
480.855.4333

FLAGSTAFF
Rabbi Dovie Shapiro
928.255.5756

GLENDALE
Rabbi Sholom Lew
602.375.2422

PHOENIX
Rabbi Zalman Levertov
Rabbi Yossi Friedman
602.944.2753

SCOTTSDALE
Rabbi Yossi Levertov
Rabbi Yossi Bryski
480.998.1410

ARKANSAS
LITTLE ROCK
Rabbi Pinchus Ciment
501.217.0053

CALIFORNIA
AGOURA HILLS
Rabbi Moshe Bryski
Rabbi Yisroel Levin
Rabbi Shlomo Bistritzky
818.991.0991

BAKERSFIELD
Rabbi Shmuel Schlanger
661.835.8381

BEL AIR
Rabbi Chaim Mentz
310.475.5311

BRENTWOOD
Rabbi Boruch Hecht
Rabbi Mordechai Zaetz
310.826.4453

BURBANK
Rabbi Shmuly Kornfeld
818.954.0070

CALABASAS
Rabbi Eliyahu Friedman
818.585.1888

CARLSBAD
Rabbi Yeruchem Eilfort
Rabbi Michoel Shapiro
760.943.8891

CENTURY CITY
Rabbi Tzemach Cunin
310.859.6060

CHATSWORTH
Rabbi Yossi Spritzer
818.718.0777

GLENDALE
Rabbi Simcha Backman
818.240.2750

HUNTINGTON BEACH
Rabbi Aron Berkowitz
714.846.2285

IRVINE
Rabbi Alter Tenenbaum
Rabbi Elly Andrusier
949.786.5000

LAGUNA BEACH
Rabbi Elimelech Gurevitch
949.499.0770

LOMITA
Rabbi Eli Hecht
Rabbi Sholom Pinson
310.326.8234

LONG BEACH
Rabbi Abba Perelmuter
562.621.9828

LOS FELIZ
Rabbi Leibel Korf
323.660.5177

MALIBU
Rabbi Levi Cunin
310.456.6588

MARINA DEL REY
Rabbi Danny Yiftach
Rabbi Mendy Avtzon
310.859.0770

MILL VALLEY
Rabbi Hillel Scop
415.381.3794

MISSION VIEJO
Rabbi Zalman Aron Kantor
949.770.1270

MONTEREY
Rabbi Dovid Holtzberg
831.643.2770

MT. OLYMPUS
Rabbi Sholom Ber Rodal
323.650.1444

NEWHALL
Rabbi Elchonon Marosov
661.254.3434

NEWPORT BEACH
Rabbi Reuven Mintz
949.721.9800

NORTH HOLLYWOOD
Rabbi Nachman Abend
818.989.9539

NORTHRIDGE
Rabbi Eli Rivkin
818.368.3937

PACIFIC PALISADES
Rabbi Zushe Cunin
310.454.7783

PASADENA
Rabbi Chaim Hanoka
626.564.8820

RANCHO CUCAMONGA
Rabbi Sholom B. Harlig
909.949.4553

RANCHO PALOS VERDES
Rabbi Yitzchok Magalnic
310.544.5544

REDONDO BEACH
Rabbi Dovid Lisbon
310.214.4999

ROSEVILLE
Rabbi Yossi Korik
916.677.9960

SACRAMENTO
Rabbi Mendy Cohen
916.455.1400

S. BARBARA
Rabbi Yosef Loschak
805.683.1544

S. CLEMENTE
Rabbi Menachem M. Slavin
949.489.0723

S. CRUZ
Rabbi Yochanan Friedman
831.454.0101

S. DIEGO
Rabbi Motte Fradkin
858.547.0076

S. FRANCISCO
Rabbi Peretz Mochkin
415.571.8770

S. MONICA
Rabbi Boruch Rabinowitz
310.394.5699

S. RAFAEL
Rabbi Yisrael Rice
415.492.1666

S. ROSA
Rabbi Mendel Wolvovsky
707.577.0277

SIMI VALLEY
Rabbi Nosson Gurary
805.577.0573

STOCKTON
Rabbi Avremel Brod
209.952.2081

STUDIO CITY
Rabbi Yossi Baitelman
818.508.6633

TEMECULA
Rabbi Yitzchok Hurwitz
951.303.9576

THOUSAND OAKS
Rabbi Chaim Bryski
805.493.7776

TUSTIN
Rabbi Yehoshua Eliezrie
714.508.2150

VENTURA
Rabbi Yakov Latowicz
Mrs. Sarah Latowicz
805.658.7441

WEST HILLS
Rabbi Avrahom Yitzchak Rabin
818.337.4544

YORBA LINDA
Rabbi Dovid Eliezrie
714.693.0770

COLORADO
ASPEN
Rabbi Mendel Mintz
970.544.3770

BOULDER
Rabbi Pesach Scheiner
303.494.1638

COLORADO SPRINGS
Rabbi Moshe Liberow
719.634.2345

DENVER
Rabbi Yossi Serebryanski
303.744.9699

HIGHLANDS RANCH
Rabbi Avraham Mintz
303.694.9119

LONGMONT
Rabbi Yaakov Dovid Borenstein
303.678.7595

VAIL
Rabbi Dovid Mintz
970.476.7887

WESTMINSTER
Rabbi Benjy Brackman
303.429.5177

CONNECTICUT
BRANFORD
Rabbi Yossi Yaffe
203.488.2263

GLASTONBURY
Rabbi Yosef Wolvovsky
860.659.2422

GREENWICH
Rabbi Yossi Deren
Rabbi Menachem Feldman
203.629.9059

LITCHFIELD
Rabbi Yoseph Eisenbach
860.567.3609

NEW LONDON
Rabbi Avrohom Sternberg
860.437.8000

ORANGE
Rabbi Sheya Hecht
Rabbi Adam Haston
203.795.5261

RIDGEFIELD
Rabbi Sholom Y. Deitsch
203.748.4421

SIMSBURY
Rabbi Mendel Samuels
860.658.4903

STAMFORD
Rabbi Yisrael Deren
Rabbi Levi Mendelow
203.3.CHABAD

WESTPORT
Rabbi Yehuda L. Kantor
Mrs. Dina Kantor
203.226.8584

WEST HARTFORD
Rabbi Yosef Gopin
Rabbi Shaya Gopin
860.659.2422

DELAWARE
WILMINGTON
Rabbi Chuni Vogel
302.529.9900

FLORIDA
AVENTURA
Rabbi Laivi Forta
Rabbi Chaim I. Drizin
305.933.0770

BAL HARBOUR
Rabbi Mendy Levy
305.868.1411

BOCA RATON
Rabbi Moishe Denberg
Rabbi Zalman Bukiet
561.417.7797

EAST BOCA RATON
Rabbi Ruvi New
561.417.7797

BOYNTON BEACH
Rabbi Yosef Yitzchok Raichik
561.732.4633

BRADENTON
Rabbi Menachem Bukiet
941.388.9656

BRANDON
Rabbi Mendel Rubashkin
813.657.9393

COCONUT CREEK
Rabbi Yossi Gansburg
954.422.1987

CORAL GABLES
Rabbi Avrohom Stolik
305.490.7572

DEERFIELD BEACH
Rabbi Yossi Goldblatt
954.422.1735

DELRAY BEACH
Rabbi Sholom Ber Korf
561.496.6228

FORT LAUDERDALE
Rabbi Yitzchok Naparstek
954.568.1190

FORT MYERS
Rabbi Yitzchok Minkowicz
Mrs. Nechama Minkowicz
239.433.7708

HOLLYWOOD
Rabbi Leizer Barash
954.965.9933

Rabbi Zalman Korf
Rabbi Yakov Garfinkel
954.374.8370

KENDALL
Rabbi Yossi Harlig
305.234.5654

KEY BISCAYNE
Rabbi Yoel Caroline
305.365.6744

KEY WEST
Rabbi Yaakov Zucker
305.295.0013

MIAMI BEACH
Rabbi Zev Katz
305.672.6613

Rabbi Aron Rabin
Rabbi Mendy Halberstam
305.535.0094

NAPLES
Rabbi Fishel Zaklos
239.262.4474

NORTH MIAMI BEACH
Rabbi Moishe Kievman
305.770.1919

ORLANDO
Rabbi Yosef Konikov
407.354.3660

PALM BEACH GARDENS
Rabbi Dovid Vigler
561.215.0404

PARKLAND
Rabbi Mendy Gutnik
954.796.7330

PINELLAS COUNTY
Rabbi Shalom Adler
727.789.0408

S. PETERSBURG
Rabbi Alter Korf
727.344.4900

SARASOTA
Rabbi Chaim Shaul Steinmetz
941.925.0770

SOUTH PALM BEACH
Rabbi Leibel Stolik
561.889.3499

SUNNY ISLES BEACH
Rabbi Yisrael Baron
CLASSES IN ENGLISH
305.792.4770

Rabbi Alexander Kaller
CLASSES IN RUSSIAN
305.803.5315

TALLAHASSEE
Rabbi Schneur Zalmen Oirechman
850.523.9294

VENICE
Rabbi Sholom Ber Schmerling
941.493.2770

WALNUT CREEK
Rabbi Zalman Korf
954.374.8370

WESTON
Rabbi Yisroel Spalter
Rabbi Yechezkel Unsdorfer
954.349.6565

WEST PALM BEACH
Rabbi Yoel Gancz
561.659.7770

GEORGIA
ALPHARETTA
Rabbi Hirshy Minkowicz
770.410.9000

ATLANTA
Rabbi Yossi New
Rabbi Isser New
404.843.2464

ATLANTA: INTOWN
Rabbi Eliyahu Schusterman
Rabbi Ari Sollish
404.898.0434

GWINNETT
Rabbi Yossi Lerman
678.595.0196

MARIETTA
Rabbi Ephraim Silverman
Rabbi Zalman Charytan
770.565.4412

IDAHO
BOISE
Rabbi Mendel Lifshitz
208.853.9200

ILLINOIS
CHICAGO
Rabbi Meir Hecht
312.714.4655

GURNEE
Rabbi Sholom Ber Tenenbaum
847.782.1800

GLENVIEW
Rabbi Yishaya Benjaminson
847.998.9896

HIGHLAND PARK
Mrs. Michla Schanowitz
847.266.0770

NAPERVILLE
Rabbi Mendy Goldstein
630.778.9770

NORTHBROOK
Rabbi Meir Moscowitz
847.564.8770

PEORIA
Rabbi Eli Langsam
309.692.2250

SKOKIE
Rabbi Yochanan Posner
847.677.1770

WILMETTE
Rabbi Dovid Flinkenstein
847.251.7707

INDIANA
INDIANAPOLIS
Rabbi Mendel Schusterman
317.251.5573

KANSAS
OVERLAND PARK
Rabbi Mendy Wineberg
913.649.4852

LOUISIANA
METAIRIE
Rabbi Yossi Nemes
504.454.2910

MARYLAND
BETHESDA
Rabbi Bentzion Geisinsky
Rabbi Sender Geisinsky
301.913.9777

BALTIMORE
Rabbi Elchonon Lisbon
410.358.4787

Rabbi Velvel Belinsky
CLASSES IN RUSSIAN
410.764.5000

BALTIMORE DOWNTOWN
Rabbi Levi Druk
410.605.0505

COLUMBIA
Rabbi Hillel Baron
410.740.2424

GAITHERSBURG
Rabbi Sholom Raichik
301.926.3632

POTOMAC
Rabbi Mendel Bluming
301.983.4200

SILVER SPRING
Rabbi Berel Wolvovsky
301.593.1117

MASSACHUSETTS
HYANNIS
Rabbi Yekusiel Alperowitz
508.775.2324

LONGMEADOW
Rabbi Yakov Wolff
413.567.8665

NATICK
Rabbi Levi Fogelman
508.650.1499

SHARON
Rabbi Chaim Wolosow
Rabbi Ilan Meyers
781.784.4269

SUDBURY
Rabbi Yisroel Freeman
978.443.3691

SWAMPSCOTT
Mrs. Layah Lipsker
781.581.3833

MICHIGAN
ANN ARBOR
Rabbi Aharon Goldstein
734.995.3276

NOVI
Rabbi Avrohom Susskind
248.790.6075

WEST BLOOMFIELD
Rabbi Kasriel Shemtov
248.788.4000

Rabbi Elimelech Silberberg
Rabbi Avrohom Wineberg
248.855.6170

MINNESOTA
MINNETONKA
Rabbi Mordechai Grossbaum
952.929.9922

ROCHESTER
Rabbi Dovid Greene
507.288.7500

MISSOURI
S. LOUIS
Rabbi Yosef Landa
314.725.0400

MONTANA
BOZEMAN
Rabbi Chaim Shaul Bruk
406.585.8770

NEBRASKA
OMAHA
Rabbi Mendel Katzman
402.330.1800

NEVADA
HENDERSON
Rabbi Mendy Harlig
Rabbi Tzvi Bronstein
702.617.0770

SUMMERLIN
Rabbi Yisroel Schanowitz
Rabbi Tzvi Bronstein
702.855.0770

NEW JERSEY
BASKING RIDGE
Rabbi Mendy Herson
908.604.8844

CHERRY HILL
Rabbi Mendy Mangel
856.874.1500

CLINTON
Rabbi Eli Kornfeld
908.623.7000

FORT LEE
Rabbi Meir Konikov
201.886.1238

FRANKLIN LAKES
Rabbi Chanoch Kaplan
201.848.0449

HILLSBOROUGH
Rabbi Shmaya Krinsky
908.874.0444

HOBOKEN
Rabbi Moshe Shapiro
201.386.5222

MADISON
Rabbi Shalom Lubin
973.377.0707

MANALAPAN
Rabbi Boruch Chazanow
732.972.3687

MEDFORD
Rabbi Yitzchok Kahan
609.953.3150

NORTH BRUNSWICK
Rabbi Levi Azimov
732.398.9492

RANDOLPH
Rabbi Avraham Bechor
973.895.3070

ROCKAWAY
Rabbi Asher Herson
Rabbi Mordechai Baumgarten
973.625.1525

TEANECK
Rabbi Ephraim Simon
201.907.0686

TENAFLY
Rabbi Mordechai Shain
Rabbi Yitzchak Gershovitz
201.871.1152

TOMS RIVER
Rabbi Moshe Gourarie
732.349.4199

WAYNE
Rabbi Michel Gurkov
973.694.6274

WEST ORANGE
Rabbi Efraim Mintz
Rabbi Mendy Kasowitz
973.731.0770

WOODCLIFF LAKE
Rabbi Dov Drizin
201.476.0157

NEW MEXICO
S. FE
Rabbi Berel Levertov
505.983.2000

NEW YORK
ALBANY
Rabbi Yossi Rubin
518.482.5781

BEDFORD
Rabbi Arik Wolf
914.666.6065

BINGHAMTON
Mrs. Rivkah Slonim
607.797.0015

BRIGHTON BEACH
Rabbi Zushe Winner
Rabbi Avrohom Winner
718.946.9833

CEDARHURST
Rabbi Shneur Zalman Wolowik
516.295.2478

DIX HILLS
Rabbi Yaakov Saacks
631.351.8672

DOBBS FERRY
Rabbi Benjy Silverman
914.693.6100

EAST HAMPTON
Rabbi Leibel Baumgarten
631.329.5800

FOREST HILLS
Rabbi Eli Blokh
Rabbi Yossi Mendelson
718.459.8432 ext.17

ITHACA
Rabbi Eli Silberstein
607.257.7379

KINGSTON
Rabbi Yitzchok Hecht
845.334.9044

LARCHMONT
Rabbi Mendel Silberstein
914.834.4321

NYC GRAMERCY PARK
Rabbi Naftali Rotenstreich
212.924.3200

NYC KEHILATH JESHURUN
Rabbi Elie Weinstock
212.774.5636

OSSINING
Rabbi Dovid Labkowski
914.923.2522

PORT WASHINGTON
Rabbi Shalom Paltiel
516.767.8672

RIVERDALE
Rabbi Levi Shemtov
718.549.1100

ROCHESTER
Rabbi Nechemia Vogel
585.271.0330

ROSLYN
Rabbi Yaakov Reiter
516.484.8185

SEA GATE
Rabbi Chaim Brikman
Mrs. Rivka Brikman
718.266.1736

STATEN ISLAND
Rabbi Moshe Katzman
Rabbi Shmuel Bendet
718.370.8953

STONY BROOK
Rabbi Shalom Ber Cohen
631.585.0521

SUFFERN
Rabbi Isaac Lefkowitz
Rabbi Shmuel Gancz
845.368.1889

WOODBURY
Rabbi Shmuel Lipszyc
516.682.0404

NORTH CAROLINA
ASHEVILLE
Rabbi Shaya Susskind
828.505.0746

CHARLOTTE
Rabbi Yossi Groner
Rabbi Shlomo Cohen
704.366.3984

RALEIGH
Rabbi Aaron Herman
919.637.6950

RALEIGH
Rabbi Pinchas Herman
Rabbi Sholom Ber Estrin
919.847.8986

OHIO
BEACHWOOD
Rabbi Yossi Marosov
216.381.4736

BLUE ASH
Rabbi Yisroel Mangel
513.793.5200

COLUMBUS
Rabbi Areyah Kaltmann
Rabbi Levi Andrusier
614.294.3296

DAYTON
Rabbi Nochum Mangel
Rabbi Dr. Shmuel Klatzkin
937.643.0770

TOLEDO
Rabbi Yossi Shemtov
419.843.9393

OKLAHOMA
OKLAHOMA CITY
Rabbi Ovadia Goldman
405.524.4800

TULSA
Rabbi Yehuda Weg
918.492.4499

OREGON
PORTLAND
Rabbi Moshe Wilhelm
Rabbi Mordechai Wilhelm
503.977.9947

PENNSYLVANIA
AMBLER
Rabbi Shaya Deitsch
215.591.9310

BALA CYNWYD
Rabbi Shraga Sherman
610.660.9192

CLARKS SUMMIT
Rabbi Benny Rapoport
570.587.3300

DEVON
Rabbi Yossi Kaplan
610.971.9977

Doylestown
Rabbi Mendel Prus
215.340.1303

Newtown
Rabbi Aryeh Weinstein
215.497.9925

Philadelphia: Center City
Rabbi Yochonon Goldman
215.238.2100

Pittsburgh
Rabbi Yisroel Altein
412.422.7300 ext. 269

Pittsburgh: South Hills
Rabbi Mendy Rosenblum
412.278.3693

Reading
Rabbi Yosef Lipsker
610.921.2805

Rydal
Rabbi Zushe Gurevitz
215.572.1511

SOUTH CAROLINA
Columbia
Rabbi Hesh Epstein
803.782.1831

TENNESSEE
Bellevue
Rabbi Yitzchok Tiechtel
615.646.5750

Memphis
Rabbi Levi Klein
901.766.1800

Knoxville
Rabbi Yossi Wilhelm
865.588.8584

TEXAS
Houston
Rabbi Moishe Traxler
Rabbi Dovid Goldstein
713.774.0300

Houston: Rice University Area
Rabbi Eliezer Lazaroff
Rabbi Yitzchok Schmukler
713.522.2004

Plano
Rabbi Mendel Block
Rabbi Yehudah Horowitz
972.596.8270

S. Antonio
Rabbi Chaim Block
Rabbi Yossi Marrus
210.492.1085

UTAH
Salt Lake City
Rabbi Benny Zippel
801.467.7777

VERMONT
Burlington
Rabbi Yitzchok Raskin
802.658.5770

VIRGINIA
Alexandria/Arlington
Rabbi Mordechai Newman
703.370.2774

Fairfax
Rabbi Leibel Fajnland
703.426.1980

Norfolk
Rabbi Aaron Margolin
Rabbi Levi Brashevitzky
757.616.0770

Richmond
Rabbi Dr. Shlomo Pereira
804.740.2000

Tysons Corner
Rabbi Levi Deitsch
703.356.3451

WASHINGTON
Bellevue
Rabbi Mordechai Farkash
Rabbi Sholom Elishevitz
425.957.7860

Olympia
Rabbi Cheski Edelman
360.584-4306

Seattle
Rabbi Elazar Bogomilsky
206.527.1411

Spokane County
Rabbi Yisroel Hahn
509.443.0770

WISCONSIN
Mequon
Rabbi Menachem Rapoport
262.242.2235

Milwaukee
Rabbi Mendel Shmotkin
Rabbi Shais Taub
414.961.6100

PUERTO RICO
Carolina
Rabbi Mendel Zarchi
787.253.0894

ARGENTINA
Buenos Aires
Rabbi Hirshel Hendel
5411 4807 7073

AUSTRALIA
Brisbane
Rabbi Chanoch Sufrin
617.3843.6770

Melbourne
Rabbi Schneier Lange
613.9522.8222
Rabbi Shimshon Yurkowicz
613.9822.3600

Sydney
Bondi
Rabbi Pinchas Feldman
612.9387.3822

Double Bay
Rabbi Yanky Berger
612.9327.1644

Dover Heights
Rabbi Benzion Milecki
612.9337.6775

North Shore
Rabbi Nochum Schapiro
Mrs. Fruma Schapiro
Rabbi Shmuly Kopel
612.9488.9548

AUSTRIA
Vienna
Rabbi Shaya Boas
431.369.1818 ext. 123

BELGIUM
Antwerp
Rabbi Mendy Gurary
32.3.239.6212

BRAZIL
Rio de Janeiro
Rabbi Yehoshua Goldman
Rabbi Avraham Steinmetz
21.3543.3770

S. Paulo
Rabbi Avraham Steinmetz
55.11.3081.3081

CANADA
ALBERTA
Calgary
Rabbi Mordechai Groner
403.238.4880

BRITISH COLUMBIA
Richmond
Rabbi Yechiel Baitelman
604.277.6427

Victoria
Rabbi Meir Kaplan
250.595.7656

MANITOBA
Winnipeg
Rabbi Avrohom Altein
Rabbi Shmuel Altein
204.339.8737

ONTARIO
London
Rabbi Eliezer Gurkow
519.434.3962

Niagara Falls
Rabbi Zalman Zaltzman

Ottawa
Rabbi Menachem M. Blum
613.823.0866

Greater Toronto
Regional Office & Thornhill
Rabbi Yossi Gansburg
905.731.7000

Lawrence/Eglinton
Rabbi Menachem Gansburg
416.546.8770

Midtown
Rabbi Shlomo Wolvovsky
416.516.2005

Mississauga
Rabbi Yitzchok Slavin
905.820.4432

Richmond Hill
Rabbi Mendel Bernstein
905.770.7700

BJL
Rabbi Leib Chaiken
416.916.7202

Uptown
Rabbi Moshe Steiner
647.267.8533

York University
Rabbi Vidal Bekerman
416.856.4575

QUEBEC
Montreal
Rabbi Berel Bell
Rabbi Ronnie Fine
Rabbi Leibel Fine
514.342.3.JLI

Town of Mount Royal
Rabbi Moshe Krasnanski
514.739.0770

COLOMBIA
Bogota
Rabbi Yehoshua B. Rosenfeld
Rabbi Chanoch Piekarski
571.635.8251

DENMARK
Copenhagen
Rabbi Yitzchok Lowenthal
45.3316.1850

GREECE
Athens
Rabbi Mendel Hendel
30.210.520.2880

GUATEMALA
Guatemala City
Rabbi Shalom Pelman
502.2485.0770

NETHERLANDS
Den Haag
Rabbi Shmuel Katzman
31.70.347.0222

Rotterdam
Rabbi Yehuda Vorst
31.10.466.9481

RUSSIA
Moscow
Rabbi Shneor Leider
Rabbi Yanky Klein
749.5783.8479

SINGAPORE
Singapore
Rabbi Mordechai Abergel
656.337.2189

SOUTH AFRICA
Cape Town
Rabbi Mendel Popack
Rabbi Pinchas Hecht
27.21.434.3740

Johannesburg
Rabbi Dovid Masinter
Rabbi Yossi Hecht
Rabbi Dovi Rabin
27.11.440.6600

SWEDEN
Stockholm
Rabbi Chaim Greisman
468.679.7067

SWITZERLAND
Lugano
Rabbi Yaakov Tzvi Kantor
091.921.3720

UNITED KINGDOM
Edgeware
Rabbi Leivi Sudak
44.208.905.4141

London
Rabbi Gershon Overlander
Rabbi Dovid Katz
502.2485.0770

Rabbi Bentzi Sudak
020.8800.0022 ext. 103

Leeds
Rabbi Eli Pink
44.113.266.3311

URUGUAY
Montevideo
Rabbi Eliezer Shemtov
5982.709.3444 ext. 109/110

VENEZUELA
Caracas
Rabbi Yehoshua Rosenblum
58.212.264.7011

JEWISH LEARNING INSTITUTE

THE JEWISH LEARNING MULTIPLEX

Brought to you by the Rohr Jewish Learning Institute

In fulfillment of the mandate of the Lubavitcher Rebbe, of blessed memory,
whose leadership guides every step of our work,
the mission of the Rohr Jewish Learning Institute is to transform
Jewish life and the greater community through the study of Torah,
connecting each Jew to our shared heritage of Jewish learning.

While our flagship program remains the cornerstone of our organization,
JLI is proud to feature additional divisions catering to specific populations,
in order to meet a wide array of educational needs.

THE ROHR JEWISH LEARNING INSTITUTE
is the adult education arm of Chabad Lubavitch,
a branch of *Merkos L'Inyonei Chinuch*, Lubavitch World Headquarters.

TORAH STUDIES

Torah Studies provides a rich and nuanced encounter with the weekly Torah reading. See how our primary Jewish text continues to speak with a message that is timely and fresh.

MY SHIUR
TALMUD LEARNING INITIATIVE

My Shiur's innovative and user-friendly format introduces students to the world of Talmudic debate and provides them with the skills to engage in independent Torah study.

SINAI SCHOLARS SOCIETY
IN PARTNERSHIP WITH CHABAD ON CAMPUS

This exclusive fellowship program invites a limited number of students at member campuses to participate in a rigorous eight-week course of study and special follow-up learning opportunities.

JLI TEENS
YOUNG SMART JEWISH
IN PARTNERSHIP WITH CTEEN: CHABAD TEEN NETWORK

Our interactive courses invite teens to eight weeks of relaxed social interaction, self-exploration, and serious fun as they examine their values and forge their Jewish identities.

JLI ON CAMPUS

Our campus foundational course, *Jewish Essentials*, introduces the basics of Judaism to students in eight self-contained lessons designed for maximum flexibility.

TORAH Café™

TorahCafé allows students to enjoy the excellence of JLI teaching at a convenient time and location as they listen to syndicated lectures from top-rated instructors.

National JEWISH RETREAT

The National Jewish Retreat is in a class of its own, providing rejuvenation of mind, body, and spirit and a powerful synthesis of Jewish learning and community.

ROSH CHODESH society

Founded in memory of Rebbetzin Rivkah Holtzberg, this program invites women to join together once a month for intensive textual study that is both engaging and practical.

JLI TRAINING ACADEMY

This exclusive fellowship program invites top JLI instructors to partner with their peers and noted professionals as leaders of innovation and the commitment to excellence.

the LAND & the SPIRIT
Mission to Israel

This mission brings participants to the Holy Land for an educational adventure, delving into our nation's rich past, while exploring its modern-day relevance and meaning.

NOTES

NOTES

NOTES

NOTES